# BEHIND CRIMMIGRATION

ICE, Law Enforcement, and
Resistance in America

*Felicia Arriaga*

THE UNIVERSITY OF NORTH CAROLINA PRESS
CHAPEL HILL

*This book was published with the assistance of the Authors Fund of the University of North Carolina Press.*

Designed by April Leidig
Set in Arnhem by Copperline Book Services, Inc.

Library of Congress Cataloging-in-Publication Data
Names: Arriaga, Felicia, author.
Title: Behind crimmigration : ICE, law enforcement, and
  resistance in America / Felicia Arriaga.
Description: Chapel Hill : The University of North Carolina Press,
  2023. | Includes bibliographical references and index.
Identifiers: LCCN 2022053863 | ISBN 9781469673226 (cloth ;
  alk. paper) | ISBN 9781469673233 (paperback ; alk. paper) |
  ISBN 9781469673240 (ebook)
Subjects: LCSH: U.S. Immigration and Customs Enforcement. |
  Immigration enforcement—North Carolina—History—21st
  century. | Police—North Carolina. | Intergovernmental
  cooperation—North Carolina—History—21st century. |
  Illegal immigration—Government policy—United States. |
  Noncitizens—Government policy—United States. | Racial
  profiling in law enforcement—North Carolina.
Classification: LCC JV7053 .A77 2023 | DDC 364.1/3709756—
  dc23/eng/20221129
LC record available at https://lccn.loc.gov/2022053863

Portions of the introduction and chapter 1 appeared earlier,
in somewhat different form, in, respectively, Felicia Arriaga,
"'We Can Talk to You, You're Less Radical': Reflexivity and
Developing Answerability," in "'I've Never Cried with a Stranger
Before': Pedagogies of Renewal and Research Dilemmas with/
by Undocuscholars and about Undocumented Immigrants," ed.
Denise Blum and Sophia Rodriguez, special issue, *International
Journal for Qualitative Studies in Education* 34, no. 8 (2021):
687–99; and Felicia Arriaga, "Relationships between the Public
and Crimmigration Entities in North Carolina: A 287(g) Program
Focus," *Sociology of Race and Ethnicity* 3, no. 3 (2017): 417–31.

To Mayra Arteaga Guevara, Oliver Bruno,
Akiel Denkins, and Daniel Turcios.

To those murdered by the police state and in
law enforcement custody. May you rest in power
and your families keep fighting in your memory.

# CONTENTS

# ILLUSTRATIONS

## Figures

## Tables

# ACKNOWLEDGMENTS

Fourteen years ago I went to Duke University wanting to become a lawyer. And as a first-year student, I took a junior/senior seminar on comparative race and ethnicity with Dr. Eduardo Bonilla-Silva that changed my life and facilitated my transition into sociology. Since then, I've taken plenty of classes with Eduardo, and each one has brought new experiences, challenges, and readings, and a community of race scholars ready for prime time. I hope I am finally ready for prime time, although we know that the revolution will not happen in our classrooms unless we change our approaches to be more community engaged.

To my developmental editor, Holli Bryan, you made this process easeful, and I appreciate your commitment to what I wanted this to become. To my editor at UNC Press, Lucas, thank you for believing in this project and for encouraging me to think about what's next. To my academic guides during graduate school and beyond, Hannah Gill, Mary Hovsepian, Becki Bach, and Anthony Peguero, thank you for investing time into my teaching and interdisciplinary theorizing, and for giving me so many opportunities to grow as an instructor, mentor, and scholar. To my dissertation committee, Martin Ruef, Jessi Streib, and Amada Armenta, thank you for agreeing to be part of my journey.

I've had many guides along the way. To my first sociology TAs—Michelle Christian and Trenita Childers—y'all showed me how to succeed in the department and are always there to mentor me when I need y'all. To the "older" race workshop crew (Louise, Victor, Rose, Elizabeth, Austin, Sarah, Collin, Alicia, Gloria, and Taneisha)—thank you for challenging me, for providing a space to decompress, and for being there when we need you. Before y'all became my family, I was fortunate to have a support system at the Boys and Girls Club of Henderson County that taught me the importance of friendship (Michelle, Tequia, Rosario, Diana, Cam) and being a good mentor (Mr. Kevin and Josh Queen). To the "new" race workshop crew—thank you for letting me guide the direction for many years, and I hope the space provides what you need in the coming years like it did for us. You all have a special place in my heart, and I hope we can always continue to make time during our annual meetings to reconnect.

To the UNC crew that always came to hang out with us (Willie, Atiya, and Brian)—thank you for coming to break bread whenever possible. To Willie and Brian, y'all constantly remind me what it means to dedicate myself to being and working in the south. Brian, thanks for always picking up the phone, for being there when I need you, for being a great storyteller, and for being unabashedly southern. Atiya, thank you for dealing with all my questions about activism, about academia, about life, and about everything in between.

To the amazing women (Nura, Danielle, and Yuri) struggling to figure out our duty to our families, communities, and academic lives, y'all are a constant inspiration and always down to remind these institutions of higher education that we exist and are here to challenge them. In this same vein, to the Latina Sociologist Club (Karina and Kim)—I hope I've prepared y'all for this journey ahead. And to the rest of my immediate Latina academic circle—Juanita, Laura, and Sophia—thanks for spending time with my family, for making me part of yours, and for your constant support, un abrazo! At Appalachian State, I must thank the new Latina crew that looks to me for support and who I look to for grounding, Maria, Jessie, and Nataly, thank you for giving me a community in a very white place. To Gina, Jonah, Amber, Juhee, Sarah, Belinda, and Aniseh—y'all made App a memorable experience.

I was able to dedicate some time reevaluating my career and on the book during a worldwide pandemic at Princeton University while getting to coteach with Ismail White and building community with SPEAR and Unidad Latina en Acción. Before that, I also received initial mentoring (Tanya Golash-Boza and Greg Prieto) and peer-support on the book project through the Summer Research Institute and then joined the Racial Democracy, Crime and Justice Network (RDCJN).

So many of us believe that the only secure community is an organized community, and I'm blessed to have so many people in my corner. This book is for them. Since 2019, I've also coordinated the North Carolina Statewide Police Accountability Network, and I owe so much of my abolitionist journey to those I've met in this process. To my Latinx community (Alan and the El Centro Crew, Amaryani, Bruno and the CIMA / Nuestro Centro Crew, Comunidad Colectiva, Althea, Carolina, Yazmin, Ricky, Martha, Griselda, Justin, Nayely, Chava, Tony, Raul, Jazmin, Jose, Julio, Ivanna, Ivan, Sandro, and Pablo), y'all are the reason I am able to end this chapter of my life with a stronger dedication to this movement. To the Durham Beyond Policing crew—Serena, Dee Dee, Jade, Courtney, Jose, China, Zaina, Meghan, Sijal, and Fatema; the Black Leadership and Organizing Collective—Mary, Holden, Blu, and Diego; and the abolitionist thought partners I've found along the way—Gino, Ajamu, Sunny, Bailey, Muffin: thank you for letting me grow into my voice. I owe so much gratitude to Iliana, Stefania, and Alissa, who were always excited to see drafts, watch PowerPoint presentation, and brainstorm pieces of this book.

And to all those in the crimmigration field who are building out space to be collaborative and critical of the world around us, thank you. That includes the 2015 Blurring the Border conference (Juan and Carolina); the 2017 Borders Masterclass; the 2017 SEIRN Annual Convening; the 2018 University of Tennessee–Knoxville Third Conference on Disasters, Displacement, and Human Rights (Fran, Juan, De Ann, Meghan), Kim Eberts, Jamie Longazel, Daniel Stageman, Mary Bosworth, Alpa Parmar, Yolanda Vázquez, César Cuauhtémoc García Hernández, and of course, Juliet Stumpf.

To Carlos and Collin—I couldn't have done this without y'all, especially during our transitions from grad school to assistant professors. Y'all kept me entertained, made me cry, lifted my spirits, and reminded me of how many challenges we made it through. To the six best friends that anyone could have (CC, Destani, Kyler, Ijeoma, and Chantel), who were there every step of the way, ready to support me with a shoulder to cry on, a mimosa, or a good story, thank you for always keeping it real and for all of our adventures.

And to my immediate family, this is for us. Thank you for always supporting me without questions. Many thanks to my siblings who have made it possible for me to detach enough to create family across the state who y'all are always willing to welcome with open arms. Now we get to add friends and loved ones from New York in the coming years. Many thanks to my dad, who calms my anxiety about what I study on a regular basis with his analysis and perspective. And of course, to my biggest cheerleader—my mom—who I never call enough but who still manages to lift up all my accomplishments.

# BEHIND CRIMMIGRATION

◀ ----------------------------------------------------------

In the fall of 2017, as I drove down I-85 South to Charlotte, North Carolina, I noticed a van pulled over on the northbound side of the highway with two police cars behind it and seven individuals, all of whom looked to be Latinx, walking away from the van. I took the next exit and circled back to ask them— one young woman, five men in their twenties, and an older man in his late thirties to early forties—*necesitan ayuda?* Did they need a ride anywhere or some help? As I drove them to the closest hotel—the Rodeway Inn and Suites, I learned that the driver of the van had been pulled over for speeding. He was a legal permanent resident who was eventually arrested for not having a driver's license. I also learned that they all had recently crossed the U.S.-Mexico border, intending to meet family in Maryland and New York. Hours later, I dropped off the older man in Charlotte with his family members. And I anxiously hoped that the other six would be picked up at the hotel, where they all awaited a ride from the young woman's family member, in hopes that they would eventually reach their intended destinations.

Ironically, that day I was driving to observe a related meeting that was taking place the following day in Charlotte. I was deep in my second year of fieldwork—visiting familiar places to attend program steering commit-tee meetings, performative exercises by sheriffs and Immigration and Cus-toms Enforcement (ICE) officials related to the 287(g) immigration program. This voluntary program deputizes local law enforcement to act as federal ICE agents, typically in a jail setting. More simply, local law enforcement can detect, detain, and deport unauthorized immigrants through an agreement with ICE (Nguyen and Gill 2010). The program gained popularity in North Carolina from 2006 to 2008 and once again toward the end of the Trump ad-ministration. For early meetings like the one in 2017, I would drive the night before and stay with a friend or family member. This night was no different, and fittingly, my friend was no stranger to these issues. I do not remember if it was after the meeting or later when I got back to Durham, North Carolina, that I found the small prayer card inadvertently left behind in my car (fig. I.1). The group did not or, I assume, could not carry many personal items, but this card seemed to provide the motivation and reassurance to continue the uncertain journey.

Figure I.1. Prayer card, front and back. Photo by the author.

I've kept that card in my car or in my purse ever since that day, as a small reminder of my commitment to addressing immigration enforcement. Even when I have temporarily misplaced it, the memory never fades, a memory that haunts me every time I pass the Rodeway Inn and Suites in southeastern Greensboro. That same shortness of breath and pit in my stomach return each time I pass that exit, a feeling that also occurs when we have ICE alerts across the state. Sometimes I can breathe through it, and other times, I know the only way to quiet those feelings is to drive to help my family, friends, and comrades who are fighting for a resolution. I can control this aspect of my life even while we cannot control where ICE will strike next.

More than ten years earlier, in 2008, a similar stop occurred along I-85 with a different conclusion. In that stop, Maria Chavira Ventura, a Mexican national, her three children, and a church friend were pulled over by an Alamance County sheriff's deputy for displaying a false license plate. Maria could not provide the sheriff deputy with a license and was ultimately taken to jail while her children were left on the side of the road with the church friend, who later fled, fearing deportation. Maria was eventually placed under a federal deportation order after going through the 287(g) process at the Alamance County Detention Center, where local jailers interview arrestees about their immigration status. Her children were forced to wait for their father to get a ride from a family member because he also lacked legal status, an identification document, and a driver's license. The sheriff deputy spoke very little

Spanish, making it difficult to discern whether or not he had asked Maria for permission to leave her children on the side of the road. Once the children were reunited with their father, he told reporters, "they were left abandoned in the middle of the street, it was a horrible experience for them, just horrible" (Collins 2008). The Department of Justice eventually investigated the Alamance County Sheriff's Office for racial profiling, and ICE ended the Alamance 287(g) program in 2012 because of these allegations, although this did not end the sheriff's eagerness to participate in ICE enforcement. In North Carolina, the Alamance County Sheriff's Office is infamous for immigration enforcement, but that is in just one of our state's 100 counties.

Throughout this book, I demonstrate three things: (1) the invisibility of crimmigration—the criminalization of immigration—in counties throughout North Carolina, (2) the normalization of crimmigration, and (3) what happens when communities resist. Specifically, I focus on the routine ways that law enforcement and local government agencies collaborate and communicate with ICE throughout the state, focusing on 287(g) programs, which allow deputized local law enforcement officers to act as ICE officials within local jails. The American Immigration Council (2012) explains, "Under Section 287(g) of the Immigration and Nationality Act, the Department of Homeland Security (DHS) may deputize selected state and local law enforcement officers to perform the functions of federal immigration agents. Like employees of U.S. Immigration and Customs Enforcement (ICE), so-called '287(g) officers' have access to federal immigration databases, may interrogate and arrest noncitizens believed to have violated federal immigration laws, and may lodge 'detainers' against alleged noncitizens held in state or local custody."

Moreover, the 287(g) partnership requires buy-in from a variety of local actors beyond law enforcement. First added to the Illegal Immigration Reform and Immigrant Responsibility Act in 1996, the 287(g) program became more popular after September 11, 2001, and in 2006 in North Carolina. While the response after 9/11 ushered in substantive localized immigration enforcement measures, immigrants also responded in mass. The most notable instance of this occurred after the passing of the Border Protection, Antiterrorism, and Illegal Immigration Control Act of 2005—a federal bill meant to strengthen interior enforcement and border security measures. The result? In 2006, millions of Latinxs, including many immigrants, took to the streets in what is called one of the largest civil rights demonstrations in American history (Zepeda-Millán 2017). In response to these mass protests, some scholars believe that the 287(g) programs and harsher interior enforcement were enacted to squash dissent. In North Carolina, that is unclear.

In 2015, the year I began field research, five sheriff's offices operated with 287(g) agreements: Henderson, Cabarrus, Gaston, Mecklenburg, and Wake

Counties. Called a "force multiplier," the 287(g) agreement provides an additional level of support to local law enforcement in identification processes. This interior immigration enforcement is an example of the devolution of immigration federalism or the reallocation of responsibilities to local law enforcement entities to embark on immigration enforcement matters. Although the practices ushered in after 9/11 were deemed necessary to "manage" perceived national security threats, race scholars emphasize how some immigrant groups are racialized and, therefore, subject to exclusion and subordination by those same entities that have historically subjugated other racial and ethnic groups (Saenz and Manges Douglas 2015; Golash-Boza and Hondagneu-Sotelo 2013; Vázquez 2015).

By utilizing information from five different counties, I explain the invisibility and normalization of local immigration enforcement programs over time. Initially, local governments welcomed the programs and operated them with little to no federal or local oversight. Given this freedom, the local agencies could use this tool to terrorize immigrants. Fortunately, some communities recognized this unchecked power and challenged the normalization of these partnerships.

## Why North Carolina?

Between 2006 and 2008, places like North Carolina became the testing ground for various immigration enforcement practices meant to target the increase of mostly Latinx immigrants. This corresponded with both state and federal appropriations increases for the program (Kandel 2016). By 2009, seven counties in North Carolina had adopted the program, and thirteen more were interested (Nguyen and Gill 2010). By 2012, there were sixty-three local agreements across the country, and North Carolina was the "most heavily represented" of the places applying to become 287(g) partners (Wong 2012). Whereas some applications were rejected by ICE, North Carolina counties have successfully submitted and been approved. At the beginning of my fieldwork (2015), five programs existed in North Carolina, but by the end, in 2018, two had been terminated after contentious sheriff races. As of September 2021, there were 144 local agreements throughout the country, with Florida, Texas, and North Carolina representing the largest shares in respective order.

But the introduction of these immigration enforcement programs did not come out of nowhere. Between 1990 and 2010, North Carolina's Latinx population increased dramatically. In 1990, only about 1 percent of the population identified as Hispanic (category used in the census), and by 2010, about 8 percent of the population identified as Hispanic, mostly driven by employment prospects. While larger cities attracted many Hispanics and, today, more than one in four North Carolina Hispanic residents live in two counties (Mecklenburg and Wake), rural cities and counties like those mentioned in this book have higher proportions of Hispanic residents than the state average. This population increase accounts for both undocumented and documented immigrants (Hoefer, Rytina, and Baker 2011). As a result, North Carolina is often deemed an emerging or new destination for the immigrant Latinx community (Marrow 2009; Nguyen and Gill 2010), even while more established Latinx communities, like Chicago and Los Angeles, remain at the forefront of scholarly interest.

Nevertheless, local memories exist of Mexican communities throughout the South (Weise 2015) before this period. In *Corazón de Dixie: Mexicanos in the U.S. South since 1910*, Julie Weise situates these local memories in New Orleans (1910s–30s), the Mississippi and the Arkansas deltas (1910s–30s and 1940s–60s, respectively), Georgia (1960s–2000s), and Charlotte, North Carolina (1990 onward). These memories—seemingly inconsistent with popular depictions of a new Latinx population in the area—stand in contrast to their contemporary migration patterns to other parts of the country. In the 1910s and 1920s, wartime recruitment efforts and changes to the Mexican economy encouraged migration to the United States, followed by the introduction of the Bracero program in the 1940s. In *How Race Is Made in America: Immigration, Citizenship, and the Historical Power of Racial Scripts*, Natalia Molina traces the history of Mexican immigration from 1924 to 1965 and pinpoints the complicated racial categories and scripts developed for Mexicans and increasingly for any suspected of being Mexican. These scripts continue to be used to other this population as a racialized group.

In the 1990s and early 2000s, the growth of the Latinx population resulted in a mix of attitudes and actions from the receiving communities, including but not limited to legislative measures, partnerships with ICE, and other local law enforcement measures such as targeted checkpoints. Geographer Jamie Winders (2007) highlights the overlap of growing immigration to the South and growing nativist sentiment across the United States in the post-9/11 moment. Finding that legislative actions across the South reflect anxieties related to "concerns about the social and cultural boundaries of southern communities" (920), she argues that "the growth of immigrant populations in the South has fused regional re-configurations of race and community to national imperatives of border control, in the process providing a new, and strongly legitimated, framework for tightening local communities' literal and figurative borders against an immigrant presence" (922).

These programs became more prevalent under 2017 executive orders, like the Enhancing Public Safety in the Interior of the United States Order and the Border Security and Immigration Enforcement Improvements Order, and a newer version began rolling out across the country in 2019. Border enforcement and militarization, particularly during the Trump administration, often monopolize the national immigration debate, yet increasingly, immigration enforcement has become common within the interior of the United States through additional crimmigration entities. As César Cuauhtémoc García Hernández (2015) describes, crimmigration law entities encompass both public and private entities like the Department of Homeland Security (DHS) and state and local governments; public officers and state and county prosecutors play an important role in investigations that "creates immigration law problems for people who lack US citizenship" (García Hernández 2015, 16). Of state court judges, he writes, "Not only do they oversee state criminal prosecutions, but since 2010 they have increasingly been called upon to determine whether defendants receive the type of advice about potential immigration consequences of conviction that is constitutionally required. The 6th amendment right to counsel, the Supreme Court recognized that year, obligates defense attorneys to determine whether a client is clearly going to face immigration consequences if convicted and advise accordingly" (García Hernández 2015, 16).

In his interviews with judges, sociologist Michael T. Light (2015) finds differential treatment based on noncitizenship status, indicating unequal treatment under the law. As one judge stated, "Is there an annoyance because some of these criminals are basically biting the hand that feeds them? Yes" (Light 2015, 35). Another judge specifically spoke about "cultural" divides between himself and Hispanics: "Now one of the things I've noticed from a lot of the Hispanic illegal aliens that I find here, they don't seems [sic] to have a great deal of problem in beating up their women, and that bothers me. It just seems to be a cultural thing I keep encountering. . . . So if this is your way of life, I'm probably gonna hurt you" (36).

And although raids and ICE visits to homes and workplaces are also entering into the popular understanding of immigration enforcement, this distracts from a more systematic approach that ICE takes, one that functions through an already present system: the use of local law enforcement and the unchecked power they are granted by local governing bodies. Moreover, little is known about the pioneering role of actors such as Mecklenburg sheriff Jim Pendergraph, the North Carolina Sheriffs' Association, and the North Carolina Police Chiefs Association in introducing and advocating for more localized models of immigration enforcement in both North Carolina and beyond. The *Raleigh News and Observer* probably said it best in an October 18, 2007, article, "N.C. Leads in Immigrant Crackdown," which highlighted the influence of sheriffs and police chiefs and how they did not the need to pass "controversial municipal ordinances that crack down on illegal immigrants, their employers, and their landlords. . . . Eighteen law enforcement agencies in North Carolina, more than any other state, have asked to join a program that would allow them to check the immigration status of those they arrest and jail" (Collins 2007). Richard Rocha, spokesperson for ICE, also noted North Carolina's leadership, noting how the state pushed ICE to create a task force to best utilize North Carolina sheriff and police departments.

Until recently, the sheriff's role in immigration enforcement—collaborating with ICE—has gone unchallenged, yet many localities in North Carolina have a longer history of setting some parameters and constructing precedents to work with ICE for not only other counties within the state but also other states. There were also often hidden financial aspects. Vargas and McHarris (2017) describe the financial relationship whereby federal assistance is adopted as a response to a perceived racial threat, yet this neglects the role individuals have in advocating for this funding. That relationship is clear in North Carolina, where former Mecklenburg County sheriff Jim Pendergraph "was hired in 2007 to head up ICE's Office of State and Local Coordination in part to oversee the 287(g) process nationally" (Coleman 2012). In 2006, Sheriff Pendergraph became the first sheriff east of California (where more immigrants lived) to adopt a 287(g) program. The December 10, 2006, issue of the *Charlotte Observer* noted of Pendergraph, "He is a bit of a rising star in immigration circles, one who chastised congressmen this summer about illegal immigration, which quickly brought him some national press, which quickly brought him hundreds of e-mail messages from across the U.S.—'none of them negative,' he says." The article further described him this way: "He is 56 years old, a Mecklenburg native, a Democrat because that's what his family has always been, a suit-and-tie professional with a soft drawl that would fit behind any small-town sheriff's desk. In Charlotte, he is one of his county's most popular public figures, a winner of seven consecutive elections, with a reputation around the courthouse as an effective administrator and something of an innovator, someone willing to see criminals for more than their crimes" (St. Onge 2006).

A year earlier, Pendergraph learned of the 287(g) program at a Sheriffs' Association meeting from a California sheriff. According to reports from the first few months of North Carolina's program, about 120 unauthorized immigrants were being arrested each month. By November 2006, not only were the results drawing praise from others in North Carolina, but also Julie Myers, assistant secretary of the Department of Homeland Security, also weighed in. "That success, frankly, has triggered interest through the country," she said (*Charlotte Observer* 2006).

Mirroring Pendergraph's approach, U.S. representative Sue Myrick, a Charlotte Republican, would often travel to Washington, D.C., to lobby for various immigration enforcement programs and partnerships, including a new detention facility in 2007 (Wootson and Helms 2007). Moreover, the U.S. Department of Justice announced around the same time that an immigration court would open in Charlotte in 2008. Both Pendergraph and Myrick then turned their focus to determining immigration status throughout the prison system (Achenbaum 2007a). Myrick said her goal was to have all North Carolina County jails and state prisons—and eventually all prisons around the country—looking for immigrants. The state secretary of correction responded that they already used "the most efficient and effective way" to screen for immigrants (Achenbaum 2007b). But Myrick's efforts were not only directed at Latinx immigrants; instead she boldly sought to demonize and other many communities. "Her critics accused her of fomenting hate against immigrant and Muslim communities. She penned the foreword to a book—'Muslim Mafia'—whose researchers called Islam a disease. Citing the book, she joined other Republicans in 2009 calling for an investigation of the Council on American-Islamic Relations, a pro-Islam nonprofit, accusing it of planting 'spies' in national-security committees to shape legislative policy" (Ordonez 2012).

In 2007, Pendergraph left his post as sheriff to head ICE's Office of State and Local Coordination. He eventually left this position shortly thereafter amid a suspected controversy between himself and U.S. representative David Price. He left the task force with high praise from ICE spokesperson Rocha: "Sheriff Pendergraph's relationships with local law enforcement agencies across the country has been an asset for ICE as the agency's first director of the office of state and local coordination" (Ordonez 2008). In 2012, Pendergraph ran for Congress to replace Myrick, receiving backing from Sheriff Joe Arpaio—the "toughest" sheriff in America known for dehumanizing immigrants—who told a reporter: "When Pendergraph was with the federal government, he praised the operations in Maricopa. Arpaio never forgot his help" (Bethea 2012). By March 15, 2011, all one hundred counties in the state had implemented the Secure Communities program—a biometric fingerprinting screening program that allows for information to be shared among various local, state, and federal agencies. According to an ICE report on "activated" Secure Communities participating areas, "As part of the Secure Communities strategy, ICE is leveraging a federal biometric information sharing capability to quickly and accurately identify aliens in law enforcement custody." Although, the federal government would begin to scale back the 287(g) program in 2012, this was not the case in North Carolina.

Pendergraph's influence would then shape the North Carolina Sheriffs' Association's (NCSA) proactive stance on local involvement in immigration enforcement. Although Abigail Fisher Williams (2018) finds that most bureaucrats and public officials often will choose more accommodating immigration policies, these issue entrepreneurs—individuals who become champions for a cause—ensured that this did not occur. Each year, the North Carolina Sheriffs' Association publishes a legislative report containing information about legislative proposals of interest, legislative proposals they oppose, and legislative proposals they support. In 2007, the North Carolina state legislature set aside funding for the 2007 Illegal Immigration Project / Sheriffs Immigration Enforcement Agreement, also known as House Bill 1950. Sponsored by House representatives Marian McLawhorn (Pitt County), Van Braxton (Greene, Lenoir, and Wayne), Ray Warren (Mecklenburg), and Joseph Kiser (Lincoln), this bill moved funds from the General Fund to the Governor's Crime Commission of the Department of Crime Control and Public Policy, allocating $750,000 for the fiscal year 2007–8. For the 2008–9 fiscal year, they also allocated $1 million to the North Carolina Sheriffs' Association to provide technical assistance and advice for the 287(g) program and to sheriffs seeking to negotiate a memorandum of understanding (MOU), as well as to enable sheriffs to send personnel to training by reimbursing travel costs and attendees' salaries.

The legislative report for 2008 indicates that the NCSA was to submit a report to the General Assembly on the operations and effectiveness of the Illegal Immigration Project. This report would cover a program overview and budget, as well as a summary of the work done with funds they received. The report was to include the total number of law enforcement agencies that received funding for officer training, officers trained, and training sessions administered, as well as copies of any education and information materials that were distributed. Finally, the report would recommend ways that resources could be used to further improve the effectiveness of the project and other enforcement initiatives (NCSA 2008 Legislative Report). *Yet no report exists.* And no legislators followed up requesting this information—a trend when it comes to any legislation pertaining to the Sheriffs Association. Legislators also know what's at stake when they are dealing with the association. In 2021, the North Carolina Sheriffs' Association stepped in to change legislation regarding the release of body camera footage, and one state representative noted, "Your sheriffs' elections typically have the biggest turnout of any election in your county," pointing out the political need to go along with the sheriff association's wishes (Locke and Battaglia 2021).

The North Carolina Sheriffs' Association has somewhat changed their tone since 2008 when it comes to immigration, particularly the opportunity to build trust within immigrant communities. But the same questions of authority and oversight remain. Table I.1 shows North Carolina state legislation relating to immigration and the sheriff's association's stance on each.

Table I.1. North Carolina Sheriffs' Association legislative agendas, 2006–2021

| Year | Proposal of interest | Stance | Conclusion |
|---|---|---|---|
| 2006 | Technical Corrections Act | No outward stance | |
| | House Bill 1048: Governor's DWI Task Force Recommendations | Pushed for changes to DWI laws that would "allow for the seizure of a vehicle that is driven by a person who is guilty of committing the following three offenses at the same time: DWI, driving with no driver's license or a revoked driver's license, and driving with no insurance" | |
| | House Bill 2692: Support Federal Immigration Legislation | Resolution urging U.S. Congress to establish a federal immigration court in NC, making DWIs a deportable offense; urges DHS to designate 6 new counties with 287(g) status | Effective July 24, 2006 |
| | House Bill 2654: Enforce Immigration Laws | No outward stance | Not enacted into law |
| 2007 | Senate Bill 229: Legal Status of Prisoners | No outward stance | Effective January 1, 2008 |
| | House Bill 1950: Illegal Immigration Project / Sheriffs Immigration Enforcement Agreement / Funds | Supported | Not passed as legislation but $750,000 (2007–8) and $1 million (2008–9) funding allocated |
| | Senate Bill 1026: Driver's Licenses Issuance / Expiration Dates | No outward stance | |
| | House Bill 1620: Clarify Arrest Authority over Illegal Aliens | Supported | Not enacted into law |

Table I.1. (*continued*)

| Year | Proposal of interest | Stance | Conclusion |
|------|----------------------|--------|------------|
| 2007 | $750,000 grant to the NCSA to provide assistance to sheriff's offices concerning the 287(g) program | Supported | |
| 2008 | Senate Bill 1955: Limited Release from Prison for Deportation | No outward stance | Effective August 8, 2008 |
| | $600,000 to the Governor's Crime Commission to contract with NCSA to provide NC sheriffs with technical assistance and training associated with immigration enforcement | Supported | |
| 2009 | $150,000 to the Governor's Crime Commission to contract with the NCSA for immigration enforcement services | Supported | |
| 2010 | Senate Bill 1242: Clarifying Changes to General Statutes, removing the requirement to annually report the number of Illegal Alien Queries | No outward stance | |
| 2011 | House Bill 36: Employers and Local Government Must Use E-Verify | No outward stance | Effective October 1, 2011 |
| 2013 | House Bill 786: RECLAIM Act | No outward stance | Vetoed by governor, veto override report findings no later than March 1, 2014 |
| 2015 | House Bill 318: Protect North Carolina Workers Act | Not supported, advocated against identification provisions | Enacted but pieces pertaining to local law enforcement identification practices eliminated |
| 2015 | House Bill 119: GSC Technical Corrections 2015 | No outward stance | Amended House Bill 318, effective October 1, 2015 |

Table I.1. (*continued*)

| Year | Proposal of interest | Stance | Conclusion |
|------|---------------------|--------|-----------|
| 2019 | House Bill 135: Enjoin Sanctuary Ordinances | Opposed then supported | Not enacted into law |
| | Senate Bill 341: Government Immigration Compliance | Opposed then supported | Not enacted into law |
| | House Bill 370: Require Cooperation with ICE Detainers | Initially against then in support | Vetoed by governor |
| 2021 | Senate Bill 101: Sheriffs to Cooperate with ICE 2.0 | Supported | Was to be determined in 2022 short session |

Actors in North Carolina were early adopters of localized immigration enforcement programs, representing a large share of the 287(g) programs nationwide, and it is in this state that questions of jurisdiction and local authority came to a head, most notably in the 2018 local sheriff elections. Looking at one of the local-level partnerships, the 287(g) program, this book examines this criminalization of immigration law and procedure, or "crimmigration" (Stumpf 2006) in the southeast, which is considered a "new immigrant destination," in order to explore how local law enforcement and other public officials frame interactions with Latinxs and Latinx immigrants. I emphasize how this system interacts with immigration policies to create a form of racialized social control different than that targeted at the "criminal black man" (Russell-Brown 2009), yet still subject to antiterrorism (i.e., anti-Muslim) tactics (Saenz and Manges Douglas 2015). In order to better trace local governance structures, I focus on how local law enforcement partners with immigration authorities in five counties (Henderson, Cabarrus, Gaston, Mecklenburg, and Wake) within North Carolina operating with a 287(g) program.

Immigration and race scholars focus on the differences between traditional and new immigrant destinations, often suggesting that locations with a longer history of immigrants and immigrant organizing have more progressive policies regarding immigration enforcement. Much of that research also suggests that Democratic-controlled areas should also see more progressive policies. In this book, however, I argue that ICE practices—an additional social control mechanism—are similar and normalized across localities, except when there is community resistance. I show that city councils, county commissioners, and the occasional appointed commission also act as crimmigration entities, which further allows for the devolution of immigration federalism. Whereas many scholars focus on local law enforcement and ICE officials, local officials—both elected and appointed—often have the power to usher in these local immigration enforcement partnerships, although that power does not turn into oversight as the partnership persists. Even when these local officials discussed the program in a public setting (i.e., city council and county commission meetings), program approval occurred in a "sealed-off political realm," whereby those most impacted (i.e., immigrants) are shut out of these local decision-making processes (Kalir and Wissink 2019, 34). And for those who can participate in the bureaucratic discussions about the program, a collective amnesia paired with limited accountability efforts means that they too allow for the normalization of the enforcement tactics.

That collective amnesia is upheld by the following frames: white innocence (Delgado and Stefancic 2000), white ignorance, white savior mentality (Bonilla-Silva 2014; Vera and Gordon 2003; Ross 1990), and economic interests and motivations. The term "collective amnesia," coined by Charles Mills (1997; 2007), describes an expansive definition of ignorance, which can include moral ignorance as part of a racialized moral psychology, where "whites will then act in racist ways while thinking of themselves as acting morally. In other words, they will experience genuine cognitive difficulties in recognizing certain behavior patterns as racist so that quite apart from the question of motivation and bad faith, they will be morally handicapped simply from the conceptual point of view in seeing and doing the right thing" (Mills 1997, 40).

Whites were not the only group to use these frames. As Mills (2007, 22) states, "the 'white' in 'white ignorance' does not mean that it has to be confined to white people. . . . It will often be shared by non-whites to a greater or lesser extent because of the power relations and patterns of ideological hegemony involved." In an exemplary case of when non-whites are strategically hired to implement enforcement practices, Amada Armenta (2015) points to the presence of two veteran bilingual officers in the Nashville Police Department, describing them as "El Protector." In her study, she finds that these individuals are examples of bureaucratic incorporation, where the officers operate with limited authority to address pressing concerns from immigrants or Latinxs. Although Latinx law enforcement agents were not often present in the counties I studied, four Black police chiefs were observed and/or interviewed to identify how these individuals may participate in the implementation of immigration enforcement. And as a result of the 2018 elections, seven Black sheriffs won their respective elections, many on a "pro-immigrant" and "progressive" platform (Shaffer 2018). Such bureaucratic incorporation, unfortunately, may further contribute to false beliefs and a lack of transparency of local law enforcement agencies who may transition to a more colorblind stance while serving a large minority population.

To complicate this further, even when local "welcoming" initiatives are adopted (e.g., municipal identifications, resolutions supporting immigrants, resolutions in support of Hispanic Heritage Month, etc.) they often provide local law enforcement with a blank check to continue business as usual, especially when it comes to communicating with ICE. But that blank check comes at a time when law enforcement agencies across the country are being scrutinized for their treatment of Black communities. While law enforcement agencies attempt to improve their relationships with predominantly Latinx, immigrant communities, this then can distract immigrants from the broader calls for police accountability, transparency, and reform. Whereas immigration enforcement is often framed as an issue impacting only one's own community, to topple the 287(g) program, some communities came together across racial divides to see the similarities in their efforts for police reforms. But why was this the case in some places and not others? In this book, I set out to answer this question along with the following: Why were these programs so popular in North Carolina? How were these programs initially negotiated? Who was involved? How were they maintained over the past ten years? How do they interact with other ICE partnerships and state-level legislation? And how might they end?

## Coming Home

I began my academic field research about two years prior to picking up these strangers in 2017. However, I unknowingly entered the field when I was born in 1990 in Hendersonville, North Carolina, a small town outside of Asheville. I say "unknowingly" because I continue to dive into the history that situates both my family and the wider Latinx immigrant community within an immigration policy regime (Aranda, Menjívar, and Donato 2014). My family lives in Henderson County, in western North Carolina, where my family migrated in the early 1990s after moving back and forth between North Carolina and Florida, along with many other families looking for work picking, among other things, apples and oranges. My dad was born in Mexico, and my mom was born along the Texas side of the southern U.S. border. For my mom, who spent part of my childhood as a single mother, it would prove difficult to maintain close connections to both family and Mexican traditions.

I do not recall the first time I feared the *poli-migra*, or what a community organizer described as "the multiple '*migras* [immigration enforcement]' that seem to coexist everywhere today" (Menjívar 2014), but I do know that the process of diving into the specifics of it within my hometown was an overwhelmingly jarring experience. It was like watching a terrifying history unfold right in front of our eyes. And yet discussions at many of my family meals remind me that these enforcement practices have been and will unfortunately continue to be part of our routine conversations, part of that cultural intuition (Bernal 1998) that draws on community memory and collective experience (Monzó 2015). Throughout my life, one story kept coming up in community conversations: sheriff employees arresting people at Latinx-serving clinics and taking them to jail for a variety of reasons. I used this collective memory to then review administrative documents and pinpoint that this probably occurred around 2008. And it continues to be a significant marker in these participants' lives.

In addition to drawing on collective memories, I collected information from five sheriff's offices and their respective county-level governing bodies in North Carolina. I initially chose these five counties—Cabarrus, Gaston, Henderson, Mecklenburg, and Wake Counties—because they were active in the 287(g) program. ICE and the law enforcement agencies call this distribution of counties across the state a "hub and spoke" model, indicating a strategic effort meant to funnel incarcerated individuals toward specific areas within the state.[1]

Table I.2 provides general information about each county's demographics. Each of the counties in the table experienced higher growth in the Latinx population than the state average, two leaned Democratic, and three had a Latinx community center. The community center is noted here as one indicator of a communal Latinx presence.

Moreover, only in these counties were "steering committee" meetings conducted by ICE, opening up opportunities to further investigate relevant administrative records related to the 287(g) program. For example, at meetings where the 287(g) program manager presented statistics about the program and community members requested additional data from another type of partnership, ICE officials would redirect the conversation. Because these were public meetings, I recorded whenever possible and transcribed the material soon after. When possible, I also followed up with community members in attendance to hear their reactions and to assist in their next steps. Table I.3 includes data collection sources from each county.

Two of these localities—Henderson and Mecklenburg Counties—underwent community input in the process of adopting the 287(g) program, and the other three did not. I interviewed and observed both deputized (those formally trained as ICE officers) and nondeputized law enforcement officers and local bureaucrats in order to broaden my understanding of the roles these entities play in crimmigration. The archival data retroactively collected for

Table I.2. North Carolina county-level characteristics, 1990–2016

| County | Percentage change in Latinx population (1990–2010) | Percentage change in Latinx population (2000–2014) | Percentage of county population (2014) | Political leaning* (2016) | Latinx Community Center? |
|---|---|---|---|---|---|
| Cabarrus | 1,271 | 190 | 10 | Republican (58.5%) | No |
| Gaston | 562 | 136 | 6 | Republican (64.8%) | No |
| Henderson | 477 | 126 | 10 | Republican (62.6%) | Yes |
| Mecklenburg | 570 | 186 | 13 | Democrat (63.3%) | Yes |
| Wake | 530 | 193 | 10 | Democrat (58.4%) | Yes |
| State | 943 | 111 | 9% of state | Republican (50.5%) | |

*Sources*: "Demographic and Economic Profiles of Hispanics by State and County, 2014," Pew Research Center, www.pewhispanic.org/states/state/nc/ (accessed August 4, 2022); "2016 North Carolina Presidential Election Results," Politico, December 13, 2016, www.politico.com/2016-election/results/map/president/north-carolina/.

*Winning party in the 2016 presidential election.

this analysis comes from all five counties from the years 2006–18. This information consisted of county commissioner meetings, city council documents when applicable, and annual budgets. A close reading of these documents revealed a variety of information, including details regarding the adoption of the 287(g) program, responses from community members, requests for more information throughout the ten years of the program, and financial exchanges between ICE and the county and local law enforcement agencies.

For this book, I also sought to better operationalize ICE collaboration through a multistage process of reviewing previous measures, synthesizing administrative records and observing participants from 2015 to the present. It was clear that local immigration enforcement was happening outside of the 287(g) programs, but often this took center stage. I group some immigration enforcement by the crimmigration entity and level of government, meaning that the three major categories are federal, state, and local.[2] These dimensions then represent the ways that local law enforcement communicates,

Table I.3. Data-collection sources across counties

| County | Public archival data | Interview data | Public meetings/events |
|---|---|---|---|
| Henderson | Blue Ribbon Committee on Illegal Immigration (2007), county commissioner meetings (2006–16), MOU, county budget documents (2006–18) | Blue Ribbon Committee members, county officials, sheriff personnel | 287(g) steering committee meeting (only participant), community meeting, sheriff information session (2015) |
| Gaston | County commissioner meetings (2006–16), MOU, county budget documents (2006–18) | | 2015 and 2016 287(g) steering committee meeting (only participant) |
| Mecklenburg | County commissioner meetings (2006–16), Mayor's Immigration Study Commission (2006–7), MOU, county budget documents (2006–18) | Community organization, Immigration Study Commission member | 2015 and 2016 287(g) steering committee meetings |
| Wake | County commissioner meetings (2006–16), MOU, County budget documents (2006–18) | Community members | 2015 and 2016 287(g) steering committee meetings |
| Cabarrus | Visioning meeting of county commissioners (2007), county commissioner meetings (2006–16), MOU, county budget documents (2006–18) | | 2015 and 2016 287(g) steering committee meeting (only participant) |

*Note*: Other sources included correspondence with 287(g) program managers in North Carolina and the southern region communications director (spokesman) with U.S. Immigration and Customs Enforcement.

collaborates, and exchanges money with ICE sometimes only after the approval of local elected officials. Immigration enforcement should be operationalized and discussed as a spectrum of communication, collaboration, and financial exchanges, including indirect collaboration through identification procedures and protocols pre–jail entry, technology usage, deputized staff, reimbursement funding, honoring of detainer or ICE hold requests, additional intergovernmental agreements, participation in joint agency task forces, and special conditions for collaboration and communication.

I also spent time at a variety of meetings as a participant observer, including 287(g) steering committee meetings and additional follow-up meetings and rallies with community members. Some of this time—over the course of three years—was also spent attending other meetings like those hosted by the Faith Action ID Network (an initiative to provide identification documents to individuals unable to obtain government-issued identification) to learn more about law enforcement perspectives. And again and again, community members also let law enforcement know both their fears of ICE enforcement and collaborative efforts with the agencies represented. Once I had collected my field notes, interviews, and archival resources, I use a modified grounded-theory approach for coding to identify analytic themes and to organize and analyze the information. For most of quoted material in the book, I do not identify the speaker by name, unless it was at a public meeting. If the name is not attached to a statement, then I indicate what agency or community organization the person represented. In this book, I am unable to reconstruct the full stories of community members, and I also did not want to possibly add to any future retaliation—a phenomenon that occurred more frequently under the Trump administration (Pinto 2020).

## Plan of the Book

Chapter 1 provides a historical overview of the 287(g) partnership between local law enforcement and ICE in five counties throughout the state: Henderson, Cabarrus, Gaston, Mecklenburg, and Wake, focusing on the initial implementation period of 2006–8 when officials explicitly voiced their intentions for these programs. Previous research typically does not describe and assess how city and county governments participated in the local immigration enforcement adoption processes in various localities. I also begin to sketch out which government agencies and offices may act as crimmigration entities—constructing and carrying out the day-to-day functions of immigration enforcement, in both indirect and direct manners. In addition, I also highlight the explicitly racist intentions of local actors, who have continued to influence these debates in the current period. In this chapter, I find that, except when 287(g) steering committee meetings began occurring in North Carolina (2015 onward), the county governments provided the only, albeit limited, public forum to usher in these partnerships between 2006 and 2008. In other words, these programs began without consultation with the communities that would be impacted and instead relied on a select group of outspoken, mostly white, officials.

Chapter 2 confronts the idea that local law enforcement engagement in immigration enforcement is categorized as a binary engagement, where agencies either do or do not participate in enforcement practices, where the former is often defined only by more intrusive enforcement practices characteristic of 287(g) programs. Yet this simplistic understanding distracts from other forms of communication, collaboration, and financial exchanges with ICE. This chapter may resonate most with those efforts that are provoking backlash for ending one partnership and are now experiencing ICE pivot to more aggressive tactics in another arena. Changing local ICE involvement is possible, but we must know where to start.

Chapter 3 describes how stakeholders in the criminal-legal system in these counties, namely city and county representatives, play a role or do not fully understand their role in the adoptions of such localized immigration policies, particularly when it comes to financial oversight. This then allows for the *persistence of the* 287(g) *program*. Moreover, these policy changes initiated almost ten years ago have become normalized and gone unchallenged as part of legal and state violence (Menjívar and Abrego 2012a) directed at Latinxs and Latinx immigrants alike in locales where 287(g) programs were adopted. And because many immigrants were unable to participate in these political processes, those most impacted were missing from the political realm.

Chapters 4 and 5 cover the different trajectories of these five counties as increased public attention—resulting from 287(g) steering committee meetings that began in 2015—revived initial concerns during what Keeanga Yamahtta Taylor (2021) calls "Trump's White-Power Presidency" sparked additional scrutiny. In Chapter 4 I review why the programs persist in three (Henderson, Cabarrus, and Gaston) of the five counties that had 287(g) programs in 2015. Although, political scientists refer to the lack of accountability efforts that persist beyond election cycles as "rational ignorance," this chapter fuses this notion with the understanding of a "collective amnesia" that works to obscure the racist beginnings of local law enforcement partnerships. Gaston and Cabarrus continue to operate with little to no community pushback. Henderson County, on the other hand, is undergoing pushback from local and state challengers and has ultimately adopted a more middle-of-the-road solution by creating the position of a Latinx liaison. In chapter 5, "Melting ICE," I focus on how communities ended the 287(g) program. Sheriffs in Mecklenburg and Wake Counties lost their reelections in 2018, opening the door for the newly elected sheriffs who promised to end the 287(g) program and other forms of ICE communication and collaboration. In these counties, the Families SI [Families Yes], 287(g) NO efforts won.

Although chapter 5 showcases a "victory" for immigrant communities, the concluding chapters highlight additional areas of interest and concern, shifting from sheriffs and county commissioners to other components of the criminal-legal system. I end with a reflection on "Opportunities from the Justice Election." Although I focus on the 2018 sheriff elections, they weren't the only focus of that election. Instead, various local and state agencies also focused on judge and district attorneys' races, emphasizing how these three offices work together within the criminal-legal system. A handful of these offices have made open commitments to support immigrant communities, providing some pathways forward that would limit ICE presence in additional sites (jails, prisons, etc.) laid out in chapter 2. Unfortunately, as a response, ICE has also taken this opportunity to further threaten and demonize the immigrant community. Moreover, ICE has stepped up public pressure on local sheriffs and within the state legislature—emphasizing the possibility of "collateral" arrests, whereby community members might be arrested even if they were not on a specific list but were encountered by ICE officials out in the field (DeGrave 2018; Feldblum 2018).

The *poli-migra* exists throughout the country, but stakeholders, particularly law enforcement, in North Carolina welcomed ICE partnerships with open arms. While this book dives into the specifics of the 287(g) program, local partnerships exist all around us with little to no oversight. For some, the impacts are monumental. For others, the pain of losing their loved ones fuels their resistance.

# CHAPTER 1

# Crimmigration Entities in North Carolina

A 287(G) PROGRAM FOCUS

Immigration and Customs Enforcement (ICE) needs local law enforcement agencies to assist in immigration enforcement, but only a handful of cities and counties would be selected to implement the 287(g) program. In 2015, five sheriff's offices participated in the 287(g) program. An initial review of administrative records reveals that ICE selected these localities based on a variety of geographic considerations, in what is called a hub-and-spoke model. This chapter describes the adoption and then initial implementation of 287(g) programs in North Carolina, focusing on Henderson County in the West; Cabarrus, Mecklenburg, and Gaston Counties in the center of the state; and Wake County in the East.

These counties, chosen because they were active in the 287(g) program in 2015, reflect the locations across the state with an opportunity for ICE, local law enforcement, and the community to engage in discussions about immigration enforcement. In this chapter, I explain how local crimmigration entities, namely county commissioners and local law enforcement, work together to respond to the Latinx immigrant threat through intergovernmental programs. Not only has the racial-threat literature taken for granted the differences between overt and covert responses to racial threat, but scholars also assume that responses by local law enforcement are consistent across demographic groups. This research bridges that gap to show the rationales in adopting an intergovernmental program for three government agencies, or rather crimmigration entities (ICE, county commissioners, and local law enforcement). Furthermore, the relationships between the entities along with the processes of adoptions are necessary to understand and study resistance efforts underway against such programs.

As indicated in the introduction, many local and state entities were in support of local immigration enforcement, but ultimately ICE would make the final decisions about a locality's participation. Therefore, the hub-and-spoke model is a thought-provoking strategy. It was not necessary for ICE to have each county in the state participate in immigration enforcement if they relied on this model. Instead, one agency could formally agree to partner with ICE as the "hub" with the surrounding agencies serving as the "spokes"—bringing detained immigrants to the hubs.

But much of this information is kept secret, even today. In some of these counties, the only public forum—local county commission meetings—in which to discuss the program's implementation occurred between 2006 and 2008. Most counties across the country hold regular monthly meetings to discuss issues related to county budgets, zoning, and so on. Meetings are often split up into working meetings—often held in the morning—and meetings held at five or six in the evening. Most also function with an opportunity for public comment on certain agenda items. Each county commission must also approve a county budget in July of each year and must also hold a budget hearing to provide an opportunity for community members to give input on the budget priorities. More detail is included in this chapter about the importance of these budget hearings, but it is important to note that although the introduction of the 287(g) program was discussed during the county commission meetings, accountability issues abounded. In 2015, ICE made a superficial attempt to possibly correct some of the growing concerns about the 287(g) program. While I could not find any official documentation regarding a directive for 287(g) programs to offer more opportunities for public engagement, every county in North Carolina with the program began holding "steering committee" meetings in 2015.

For this chapter, I describe my time as an active participant observer as well as time spent conducting formal and informal follow-up interviews with attendees at 287(g) steering committee meetings. I separate my findings into three key areas of interest. The first is the *program adoption rationale* and *program implementation*, themes I connect to initial program adoption and framing by incorporating paraphrased sections of meeting minutes from the board of commissioners in each county. The second key area is the extent to which each sheriff's office exhibited a sense of *program ownership*, which helped to delineate the role of local law enforcement, state legislation, and federal immigration enforcement authority. Last, I describe the *community relationships* with both ICE and the sheriff's office. To the last point, chapters 4 and 5 provide more details about this divergence in levels of community participation and awareness.

## Steering Committee Overview

Steering committee meetings were announced two weeks in advance, typically on the sheriff office's website. No agenda was shared, and limited details were available. A typical meeting would be structured with a program over-view, a few statistics, then time for questions.

In the steering committee meetings, presenters (usually a regional 287[g] program officer) delivered information in a consistent and formulaic man-ner, often leaving those in attendance with more questions than answers. The 287(g) program manager for North Carolina would then present the vi-sion and the following mission statement: "To improve the program over-sight, identify issues and concerns regarding the immigration enforcement activities, to increase the transparency of the program, and offer the com-munity stakeholders opportunities to communicate from a community level perspective."

The program manager then presented the number of personnel trained to implement the program in each county, the number of persons encountered and removed, and success stories from an ICE perspective. Then came time for questions and answers that varied in length and depth at each location, depending on the number of community members in attendance. In 287(g) steering committee meetings in 2015, where I was the only person in atten-dance, three out of the five meetings, I took advantage of the question-and-answer section of the presentation to ask questions of both sheriff personnel and ICE officials. In those circumstances, five to ten people were available to respond to my questions in meetings that lasted approximately thirty to forty-five minutes, ample time for me to ask about most of the topics included in my interview guides.

## Program Adoption Rationale

In each county, the 287(g) programs begin at the request of the sheriff's of-fice or of ICE or of both. In all five counties where the 287(g) program existed in 2015, local law enforcement presented the program to the board of com-missioners prior to initial adoption between 2006 and 2008. In Mecklenburg, Henderson, and Gaston Counties, county commissioner requests to better understand the impact of immigrants predated the adoption of the 287(g) program. Unfortunately, those requests resulted in studies (some more scien-tifically sound than others) showing only the negative impacts of the growing Latinx immigrant population.[1] These efforts showcased a more expansive framing of the perceived problems that immigrants brought to the commu-nities beyond the racialized criminal narrative. These proposals and reports provided recommendations in the following areas: monitoring of local fund-ing that might provide support to "illegal residents," ceasing to work with businesses employing "illegal residents," monitoring housing occupancy in rental dwellings, and so on. In most cases, in order for the sheriff's office to dedicate budgetary resources and personnel to new obligations under the 287(g) program, it was necessary for the county board of commissioners to accept the proposal; however, this did not create a sense of ownership on behalf of the board of commissioners.

Surprisingly, in the county commissioner meeting on February 20, 2008, the Henderson County sheriff candidly emphasized ICE's geographic rationale for implementing agreements with specific counties. According to the sheriff, "Henderson, Wake and Cumberland Counties were chosen because of the demographics, geographics and intensive lobbying. ICE cannot support 100 individual 287 (g) programs across the state. They are going with the 'Hub & Spoke' approach. The concept is a fifty (50) mile radius where a county would support the surrounding counties. We would be actively supporting the counties of Transylvania, Buncombe, Polk, Rutherford, Haywood, McDowell, Madison and Yancey" (Henderson County BOC 2008b). The aforementioned counties all surround Henderson County, meaning that one 287(g) program could support the surrounding sheriff agencies efforts to target, arrest, and detain immigrants. In these instances, separate transfer and/ or transportation agreements were also created. For immigrants, this meant that they were subject to racialized social control not just in one county, but in every arena of their lives. Not only does this imply a greater influence of ICE in specific areas of the state, but it also contributes to our understanding of the racialization of space where technologies of control—surveillance tactics and policing rituals directed at migrants—are implemented by local law enforcement, particularly at sites where immigrants and the places they inhabit/frequent are deemed "dangerous" (McDowell and Wonders 2009).

Some sheriffs maintained their pro-287(g) program position over the course of this intergovernmental agreement, making it possible to hear their original, often racist, intentions during the 287(g) steering committee meetings. Some of these sheriffs were intentionally targeting Latinx immigrants, a practice that they report to have changed, yet the intentions have stayed the same. That discrepancy then fuels community distrust. When the sheriff or sheriff personnel were asked about the history of the program and the rationale for adoption at a December 3, 2015, steering committee meeting, four of the five shared the following sentiment expressed by then sheriff Donnie Harrison of Wake County:

> The reason, I'll be honest with you, the reasons why I came up with 287(g) was when I became Sheriff, our jail had a lot of people in it and there were people in it that I knew that we were letting out that we didn't have a clue who they were. And it doesn't matter to me, as she said, that's the way we feel—people who have a badge on. Our job is to keep every one of

you safe and that's why I felt like, looking at the jail reports and some of the names I was seeing, and some of the people I was seeing, and some of the questions that were being asked of me, we're not sure we've got this person. We've got finger prints we can't match up anymore.

Harrison also commented on the program's usefulness in identifying individuals when he described the program to the county board of commissioners in 2008 (Wake County BOC 2008), yet there was no consistent agreement among county commissioners, sheriff personnel, and ICE in the five counties over whether or not the program would solely target criminals. Today, this debate continues, and federal directives outline deportable offenses for immigrants; but that was not as clear in the early years of 287(g) program adoption. For example, in Gaston County, then commissioner John Torbett's resolution "To Adopt Policies and Apply Staff Direction to Illegal Residents in Gaston County," which passed on November 9, 2006, included the following: "Allow County Police to partner with ICE to verify undocumented residents during any minor/major public safety infraction and if identified as undocumented, detain for deportation." Although other county commissioners and local law enforcement across field sites may not share Commissioner Torbett's sentiment, both the Gaston County Sheriff's Office and the county board of commissioners heavily dictated initial adoption.

Commissioner Torbett's comments in Gaston County also reflected participant perspectives in Henderson County. Representatives of a special committee, the Blue Ribbon Committee on Illegal Immigration, appointed by the board of commissioners in Henderson County, also desired to broaden the scope of those considered deportable by mutually recommending that "the Sheriff's department should investigate the employment record of anyone identified as an illegal alien. The identity of the employer should be noted and reported to the County Commissioners or the City of Hendersonville for appropriate action" (Henderson County BOC 2007a).

The question of "who is deportable" remains at the forefront of local and federal policy discussions. Federal guidelines sometimes include those who have criminal backgrounds while other times it is less clear. Yet most people don't know that immigration violations like crossing the border illegally are not automatically a criminal offense. In addition, people are unjustly arrested all the time and charged with criminal offenses but may not be convicted of those crimes. The initial adoption of the 287(g) programs conflated criminal and immigration violations while criminalizing and assuming culpability of Latinx immigrants even before encountering law enforcement. A 2009 report by Dr. Dora Schriro found that 66 percent of those in immigrant detention were "subject to mandatory detention" and 51 percent were felons (Schriro

2009). More importantly, Schriro found that the 287(g) program detained about 12 percent of the total number of immigrants in 2008–9, yet arrests were disproportionately of immigrants without a previous criminal record (72 percent in fiscal year 2008 and 65 percent in fiscal year 2009). While in 2015, approximately 87–89 percent of all ICE arrests were of immigrants convicted of a crime, by 2018, this percentage had decreased to 63 percent, meaning that the guidelines were again becoming more expansive to include more immigrants (Gomez 2019). These and other studies suggest that if there were federal guidelines describing the categories of individuals to deport, the deportation of both criminal and noncriminal categories of people would be considered overreaching—themes that resonated across North Carolina communities (Golash-Boza and Hondagneu-Sotelo 2013). The "priorities" for deportation in 2015 are further explained in the next section. Although the committee pinpointed the challenges in estimating the number of undocumented immigrants in the county, this particular recommendation subjects all immigrants to unnecessary scrutiny, particularly when it is carried out by a law enforcement agency eager to engage in deportation efforts.

## Program Implementation

Mecklenburg County first adopted the 287(g) program in late 2006 and early 2007, followed by Gaston, Wake, and Henderson Counties in 2007, and Cabarrus County in 2008. In addition, immigration-related recommendations accompanied the adoption and beginning of the 287(g) program in Mecklenburg, Henderson, and Gaston Counties. In those counties, community members could expect a shift in law enforcement practices while in Cabarrus and Wake Counties, this trajectory is less clear.

In interviews with community members in one county but consistent across each case study, they described the visible and overt enforcement by the sheriff's office in the initial years following adoption of the 287(g) program. This included but was not limited to reports of sheriff deputies sitting outside of the migrant health clinic and waiting to stop individuals. These reports also seem to be consistent with the number of detainers (requests from ICE to hold undocumented individuals for an additional forty-eight hours) reported by TRAC Immigration data-gathering services.[2] TRAC's Immigration Project is a unique new multiyear effort to systematically acquire very detailed information from the government, check it for accuracy and completeness, and then make it available in an understandable way to the American people, Congress, immigration groups, and others.

Information from the 2015 287(g) steering committee meeting in Henderson County further iterated this point, where out of 120 criminal encounters,

45 persons were removed, and out of 7 noncriminal encounters, 3 persons were removed. Unfortunately, for data collection purposes, reporting mechanisms and guidelines for the categories of persons to be deported changed during the course of my fieldwork, making it difficult to track the persistence of the categories of criminal and noncriminal deportations. Initially, data was split into categories of criminal and noncriminal deportations, but these shifted to hide whether deportations of those without criminal records were occurring, reclassifying the categories into three priority areas. In the fall of 2015, the North Carolina 287(g) program manager addressed the current process and newly implemented guidelines whereby criminals are identified and prioritized as various categories of threats through the Priority Enforcement Program (PEP).

Secretary of Homeland Security Jeh Johnson outlined the following three priorities in a memorandum on November 20, 2014: Priority 1, threats to national security, border security, and public safety; priority 2, misdemeanors and new immigration violators; and priority 3, other immigration violations. This memorandum (Johnson 2014) also did away with the program formerly known as Secure Communities even while pieces continued under the Trump administration. Although this memorandum was issued in 2014, the guidelines did not immediately take effect, and data is presented below with different categorizations based on this policy shift. Mirroring those ordered deported prior to the 2014 memorandum, table 1.1 indicates deportation offenses under the various priorities, including the lowest priority and thus potentially for individuals without a criminal record, for 2015.

As the table indicates, the Mecklenburg County Sheriff's Office facilitated the removal of the highest number of unauthorized immigrants (386), whereas the Wake County Sheriff's Office reported encountering the highest number of individuals (2,265). Not all those "encountered" faced deportation, regardless of the priority level they fell into, yet it is unclear why such a variation exists, particularly across counties. For example, the Gaston County Sheriff's Office had the highest overall percentage of category 1 individuals encountered and processed for removal at 89 percent. Overall, the Gaston County Sheriff's Office processed individuals for removal at high rates, greater than or equal to 70 percent, across priority categories, whereas the Wake County Sheriff's Office did not report similar rates of encounter to removal numbers.

When 287(g) officers determined that an arrestee fit the priorities outlined in the Johnson memo, this arrest was considered a "success" story, and each steering committee meeting ended with various examples of them. These always seemed a strange component of the meetings, but it was obvious that the officers were using them to justify the existence of the program, even if the stories did not include whether the immigrants were convicted for the

Table 1.1. 287(g) encounters and removal proceedings in fiscal year 2015*

| | Encounters | Removals | Percentage of removals |
|---|---|---|---|
| Cabarrus County | | | |
| Priority 1 | 56 | 20 | 36% |
| Priority 2 | 28 | 9 | 32% |
| Priority 3 | 40 | 5 | 12.5% |
| Total | 124 | 34 | 27% |
| Gaston County | | | |
| Priority 1 | 19 | 17 | 89% |
| Priority 2 | 24 | 21 | 88% |
| Priority 3 | 44 | 31 | 70% |
| Total | 87 | 69 | 79% |
| Henderson County | | | |
| Priority 1 | 19 | 15 | 79% |
| Priority 2 | 7 | 2 | 29% |
| Priority 3 | 26 | 10 | 38% |
| Total | 52 | 27 | 52% |
| Wake County | | | |
| Priority 1 | 591 | 109 | 18% |
| Priority 2 | 550 | 134 | 24% |
| Priority 3 | 1,124 | 51 | .05% |
| Total | 2,265 | 294 | 13% |
| Mecklenburg County | | | |
| Priority 1 | 499 | 168 | 34% |
| Priority 2 | 290 | 100 | 34% |
| Priority 3 | 657 | 118 | 18% |
| Total | 1,146 | 386 | 34% |
| 287(g) state total | 3,622 | 783 | 22% |

*2016–17 statistics are also available.

Table 1.2. "Success" stories

| Country of origin | Offense(s) |
|---|---|
| Honduras | Failure to appear on traffic-related charge with criminal conviction and drug trafficking, possession of a weapon, and DUI. |
| Dominican Republic | Felony burglary and entering, robbery, possession of firearm by felon, and sale of controlled substance. |
| Mexico | Driving while impaired, had criminal conviction of carrying a loaded firearm in public, and two DUIs. |
| Mexico | Felony attempted robbery, firearm, assault with a deadly weapon, and misdemeanor injury to personal property. |
| Mexico | Previously awarded 3 counts of trafficking, etc. |
| Uruguay | Federal Racketeer Influenced and Corrupt Organizations Act (RICO) Act, MS-13 gang member. |
| Jordan | Charged with breaking and entering, possession of weapons. |
| Colombia | DWI, prior convictions for 1st degree rape and assault, kidnapping. |
| Mexico | Arrested for injury to personal property, prior criminal conviction and arrest history for attempted kidnapping, attempted 2nd degree kidnapping, felony probation violation, and resisting an officer, removal order in January 2010, reentered illegally. |

offenses. Listed in table 1.2 is the country of origin and offenses, both criminal and civil, where applicable, of individuals considered success stories.

It is clear from the sample in table 1.2 that many of the encountered and deported are from Mexico and Central or South America, which further emphasizes the focus on a "Latinx threat." Unfortunately, encounter and removal data as a whole are not broken down by race, ethnicity, or county of origin. In addition, efforts to retrieve such information were not successful. These examples make it appear as though the only people processed for removal are criminals of the highest priority, yet I would assume that these examples were strategically chosen to encourage a sense of moral panic (Longazel 2013) and justification to strengthen the rationale of the program. ICE officers attempted to present stories about "criminals" in the hopes that community members would share their vision. And local law enforcement would back them up by telling community members that they were keeping the community safe from these immigrants. To some extent, these officials relied on a collective consciousness that encourages us to trust that law enforcement keeps us safe and protects us. So, it would be harder for them to garner support if they presented information about individuals who were arrested and detained for low-level driving offenses like a broken taillight.

Unfortunately, that collective consciousness prevails even when we are presented with contradictory information about law enforcement. In 2009, these sheriffs and state and local leaders had to defend the programs after a U.S. Government Accountability Office report criticized many of the agencies (GAO 2009). A 2009 report by the American Civil Liberties Union (ACLU) and the Immigration and Human Rights Policy Clinic at UNC–Chapel Hill highlighted the lack of memorandum of agreement (MOA) guidelines put in place for the programs, which should have included setting up complaint mechanisms, publicizing officials' functions, outlining how certification takes place, providing for interpreters, creating a steering committee, and potentially allowing for modification of the MOA with public input (Weeks 2009). In 2012, fifty-seven complaints made about the program in Wake County were still pending investigation by ICE (McDonald 2012).

In Henderson County, the last time program statistics were presented to the county commissioners was in August 2010, prior to a transition in the sheriff's office (Henderson County BOC 2010). In previous updates (table 1.3), the board of commissioners received additional information about the number of individuals interviewed and processed, along with their charges (see chapter 4 for more details). Not surprisingly, and consistent with similar research in other localities across the country, many of these individuals first encountered law enforcement through traffic violations, and the majority were charged with misdemeanors.

## Program Ownership

The memorandum of understanding between each sheriff's office and ICE outlines various duties and benefits for both parties, namely "to which ICE delegates nominated, trained, certified, and authorized [sheriff's office] personnel to perform certain immigration enforcement functions as specified herein." Nowhere in the agreement does responsibility fall on county or city officials, yet a representative from the board of commissioners can also sign on to the agreement. Within the steering committee meetings, the 287(g) program manager typically presented all relevant information, unless an audience member directly asked questions to sheriff personnel. A combination of the local supervisory detention and deportation officer, the southern region communications ICE director, and the acting ICE deputy field office director for the Atlanta field office was also present in the four latter meetings to field

Table 1.3. Henderson County Board of Commissioners immigration update

| Time period | Immigration statistics |
|---|---|
| July 2008–March 2009 | |
| Interviewed | 336 |
| Processed | 279 (83%) |
| Traffic (total of 183) | 77 (42%) |
| Misdemeanors | 191 (73%) |
| Felonies | 71 (27%) |
| January 2010–March 31, 2010 (from August 2, 2010, meeting) | |
| Interviewed | 63 |
| Processed | 59 (94%) |
| Traffic | 31% |
| Misdemeanors | 74 (84%) |
| Felonies | 14 (16%) |

questions. The Atlanta field office is responsible for Georgia, North Carolina, and South Carolina.

The intergovernmental aspect of the partnership was highlighted in presentations made to the county board of commissioners in the initial stages of adoption, yet at a 287(g) steering committee meeting in 2016, only a representative from the Cabarrus County Sheriff's Office suggested that another partnership was one more tool for local law enforcement. For law enforcement, this indicated an outward expression of the opportunity to diversify their current operations. And for ICE, it meant an additional agency willing to do the work that they are unable to complete. ICE's southern region communications director additionally commented:

> But what it really does from the ICE perspective is rather than having an ICE officer at a County Jail doing the processing, that by letting a local law enforcement who is already here. . . . One of the things we get all the time is why don't you focus on criminals or fugitives or things of that nature? That's put an additional ICE officer out back, eligible to be out in the community doing exactly that. So that's why, from our perspective bottom line 287(g) is an important thing. But I know we do get that question a lot, that the assumption is that local law enforcement gets additional authority.

For ICE, while the program did not grant them more authority, it made it possible for them to use their staff of ninety to one hundred federal immigration officers elsewhere in North Carolina.

Because ICE officials typically ran the steering committee meeting, program ownership became a central topic for discussion for both sheriff personnel and community members. In all these meetings, I often wondered to myself, "Who owns the program?" and "Who feels accountable for it?" On two occasions, in separate steering committee meetings, sheriff personnel asked questions of the 287(g) program manager. I initially assumed that sheriff personnel would know all the information before these presentations, so I did not expect them to also ask questions. These instances suggested a few things. Perhaps the sheriff's office did not pass on information to all personnel, and thus, perhaps these partnerships did not have much ongoing discussion in the local offices.

Only in Mecklenburg County were the sheriff personnel seated in the front of the room with the immigration officers (supervisory detention and deportation officer, southern region communications director, and the acting deputy field office director). And in Wake County, Sheriff Donnie Henderson felt compelled to make a statement and speak with audience members. Local law enforcement from the police department (aka the municipal police) were never present at these meetings. At a 2016 Gaston County Steering Committee meeting, the assistant chief deputy jail administrator commented on this in an attempt to deflect some responsibility: "They think 287(g) encounter, but they can be brought in by city police etc. for whatever charges and brought before us then it's become apparent by going through the process. In the public, they think it's the Sheriff's office are the ones going out and targeting, not really true—don't have that decision."

While they were present in the adoption of the 287(g) programs, the county boards of commissioners across all counties have not remained involved in the decision-making process, aside from managing funding requests from the sheriff and approving reimbursements from ICE. This budgetary component of the program surfaced in only a few of the public records of county budgets after initial adoption; except in Henderson County, there was no public discussion about the costs or about funds that were dedicated to the 287(g) program. In 2008, during the February and March county commissioner meetings in Henderson County, the sheriff gave the following economic rationale for the program: "This is a relief mechanism to have someone with lower offenses to at least bond out. The majority of the people that are in our Detention Center that are wanted, illegal or not, are there because they were picked up on minor offenses. Persons under arrest will be identified. Henderson County will recover all cost then some" (February 20, 2008).

In steering committee meetings, the memorandum of understanding was often discussed. In one meeting, the southern region communications director specified that no salaried positions are associated with the 287(g) program, but both sheriff's office personnel and ICE representatives described money spent by ICE to train and maintain the program in each county. In the county-specific presentation, the 287(g) program manager described those costs and highlighted the number of officers trained, ranging from fourteen to thirty-seven officers across the five counties, the most in Wake County.

Complicating this understanding of the program's financial components were county budget documents, which indicated other transactions between ICE and the county boards of commissioners. For instance, in Henderson County, an Immigration and Customs Enforcement Fund, which ranged from $745,691 in 2008 to $469,151 in 2015, was included in the annual budget. Similarly, in Gaston County, periodic reimbursements occurred, marked as "Appropriated Overtime Funds from United States Immigration and Customs Enforcement." County commissioners were often supportive of funding opportunities associated with the program and are more than likely going to support sheriff office requests, no matter the purpose. For example, county commissioners approved seed money for the program in Henderson County in the following manner:

> Commissioner Chuck McGrady made the motion that the Board support the Sheriff's efforts in this regard and authorize the recruitment of two (2) positions contingent upon the successful negotiation of an agreement with ICE officials. He further moved that the Board request that the Sheriff's Department work with the county staff to estimate the costs for any related capital needs at the Detention Center and bring those estimates back for the Board's consideration at the earliest possible date. He further moved that the Board authorize that $25,000 be taken from fund balance with the understanding that it will be reimbursed in the future as the funds flow from the ICE program. All voted in favor and the motion carried. (Henderson County BOC 2008b)

During initial adoption in Henderson County, two of the county board of commissioners did request to remain updated about the program's progress, yet no additional mentions appear in county commission documents that would suggest such oversight was taking place by the county board of commissioners, particularly during my time spent in the field. Surprisingly, that limited governance and sense of ownership was a topic of concern in the 2015 North Carolina Legislative Session and at one of the steering committee meetings. Over the span of the 2015–16 287(g) steering committee meetings, House Bill 318, the Protect Workers Act, was passed in the North Carolina

General Assembly, bringing a renewed interest in local governments' level of involvement in deterring or welcoming immigrants. Namely, two provisions in the bill instructed that cities and counties could not put limits on law enforcement agencies partnering with ICE, including related data collection regarding citizenship or immigration status. Prior to this law, no localities in North Carolina had anything remotely similar to a policy that would restrict this type of enforcement or data collection. Furthermore, it is clear from the involvement of the local governments in the acceptance and adoption of the 287(g) programs that they did in fact have the power to create similarly "pro-immigrant" policies. As previously mentioned, Henderson, Mecklenburg, and Gaston Counties all collected information about the Latinx immigrant community prior to adopting the 287(g) program. Although much of that information focused on the negative impacts of immigration, some included information on the immigrant population's contributions. But this information did not encourage the local governments into action in the same way. Whereas the localities could have initiated pro-immigrant initiatives, they instead took on only the enforcement-heavy approach.

## Nonexistent Community Relationships

Community awareness and input is not unique when we consider the administrative burdens inherent in interacting with government agencies (Herd and Moynihan 2019). Administration burden, according to Herd and Moynihan, includes learning costs (collecting information about public services), psychological costs (associated stigmas and frustrations), and compliance costs (material burdens), all of which were exacerbated for the predominately Spanish-speaking immigrants within these communities. These factors limit anyone's ability to participate in local government decisions but are important for understanding specifically for the 287(g) program because there were initial opportunities for community input.

On December 14, 2006, at the Gaston County Board of Commissioners meeting, three audience members participated in public comment. The meeting minutes note that these individuals "voiced their opposition to wording used in the recently adopted resolution, To Adopt Policies and Apply Staff Direction Relating to Illegal Residents in Gaston County, and requested the Board of Commissioners rescind the resolution" (Gaston County BOC 2006c). Aside from this public comment, most 287(g) program feedback initially was heard whenever the county appointed a committee or task force dedicated to studying the impact of immigration in their county. In those instances, representatives from the local Latinx community center in Mecklenburg and

Henderson Counties were able to represent their communities even if they encountered openly racist disagreements from other participants. Some community members, particularly through the Blue Ribbon Committee on Illegal Immigration in Henderson County, found such discussions to be combative and full of anti-immigrant rhetoric. Yet the initial stages of adoption of the 287(g) program actually provided the most opportunities for public input seen across the programs' lives, though much of this input was one-sided in favor of law enforcement.

Almost ten years later, in 2015, the program began to function with the 287(g) steering committee meetings, showcased as a public forum for community members to voice their opinions and ask questions about the program. I am not suggesting that during that ten-year time period there were not instances in these counties where questions about the program arose, but the mandate to hold the steering committee meetings obligates local law enforcement to initiate such a public forum instead of community members doing so. I am suggesting that limited opportunities for community input also display the local government's lack of outreach to immigrant communities, making it impossible for them to participate in this political realm. The steering committee meetings were typically advertised only on the sheriff's office website. Even after asking for a yearly list of the meetings, I was informed that they would be available only on each county's respective website two weeks prior to the meeting. The only outlier in this advertising was in Wake County, where a coalition of community members created their own informational materials and encouraged community members to attend. In my experiences, these meetings were not meant to encourage community participation, and intentional outreach would include requests to community-based organizations that work with immigrants.

Although community members and I asked questions about services and relationships with the immigrant community as a whole, the typical sheriff response referenced Latinxs and Hispanics. This response emphasized the population dynamics in North Carolina and an overtly racialized stereotype of those most impacted, in number, by this particular ICE partnership. Furthermore, responses to these questions described more reactive than proactive attempts to maintain these relationships, although those representatives in Henderson County did specify that a daily interpreter line was available until midnight. The reactive response is exemplified in comments from a Cabarrus County sheriff representative who, at a February 23, 2016, meeting at the Cabarrus County Sheriff's Office and Detention Center, discussed the office's initial outreach to the Latinx immigrant community that decreased over time:

Over the years, we've had, especially in the inception of the program, we naturally reached out to all organizations that we felt had some kind of brush with Hispanics/Latinos and we had more involvement in the beginning because there's probably more speculation on their behalf on how it worked, what it looked like, will we be targeted, that sort of thing. For a number of years, we had those discussions and I think that has subsided greatly for a number of reasons. First and foremost, I think it has subsided because the fear went away. After a while, they realized. I remember going on several media outlets and answering questions— open questions, live questions. It was all positive, I never received any negative response, I don't think.

In Wake and Mecklenburg Counties, the community members present at steering committee meetings alluded to previous meetings with the sheriff, and some even expressed familiarity with the services and website information. In Mecklenburg County, reporters from a Spanish-language newspaper were present and asked questions regarding the sheriff's previous policy, in which the sheriff's office website presented data about those deported. In lieu of that information being made readily available on the website, the sheriff employees indicated that the steering committee was meant to replace that type of free flowing information.

The relationship between the community members and ICE affiliates was less familiar than that with the sheriff's office, yet the deputy field officer indicated his direct work with North Carolina–specific groups such as NC DREAM Team, Jesus Ministries, and other nongovernmental organizations (NGOs). At these meetings, the deputy field officer, along with the southern region communications director, also challenged the folks in the room to encourage community members to contact local law enforcement during times of need, particularly if they might be eligible for a U-Visa or if they were a victim of domestic violence, and the latter sentiment was repeated in two separate meetings.[3] The southern region communications director directed both reporters and community members to reach out to him for data requests and then to submit public records requests in the event that he was unable to provide the relevant information.

At the 2015 Wake County Steering Committee meeting, community members disrupted the meeting and walked out to hold a rally outside. This set the tone for the subsequent 287(g) steering committee meetings in other counties. In the Wake County meeting, seventeen community members and three media outlets were present. Some of those community members attended a press conference held prior to the steering committee meeting, following their first court appearance after protesting their October 29, 2015, arrests in response to the adoption of North Carolina House Bill 318 (the Protect Workers Act). Although House Bill 318 included many provisions, one aspect of the legislation attempted to clarify the relationship between local law enforcement and ICE—a relationship that many community members in the steering committee meeting wanted to see end. To an extent, it seemed the personnel from ICE were prepared to handle such a disruption, particularly given that they attended this meeting with more individuals to handle and manage queries from the press. After the disruption, they continued responding to questions both from audience members and from media.

## Conclusion

In this chapter, I explain how local crimmigration entities, namely county commissioners and local law enforcement, work together to respond to Latinx immigrant threat through intergovernmental programs. These 287(g) agreements also allowed sheriff personnel to skirt public information requests, some of which I do not believe fall under the purview of federal-level information (i.e., requests about community-level relationships with both the immigrant and the Latinx communities). Of course, my research and requests for information are not occurring in isolation, and community organizations are taking matters into their own hands by proposing their own meetings with both sheriff and police, particularly during a time when anti-immigrant bills are being proposed each time the North Carolina Assembly reconvenes.

In January 2016, the National Day Laborer Organizing Network (NDLON), Asian Americans Advancing Justice–Asian Law Caucus (AAAJ-ALC), and the Kathryn O. Greenberg Immigration Justice Clinic at the Cardozo School of Law filed a federal lawsuit against ICE and nine other federal agencies, requesting information about the PEP. Pablo Alvarado, from NDLON described their rationale for doing so: "ICE is, once again, operating in secrecy. It's time for the nation's largest police force to come clean. PEP has failed to meet the bare minimum requirements for transparency and accountability" (NDLON 2016).

This lawsuit came after ten months of waiting for the federal agencies to fill previous Freedom of Information Act (FOIA) requests. With this in mind, these county-level steering committee meetings may be one of the only ways to begin sifting through this data while assessing both the program's goals and the compliance with deportation priorities under the PEP. Unfortunately, the 287(g) steering committee meetings are not common in other counties where the program does not exist. In other words, ICE operates in many ways in local communities, but there are not open forums operated by them to discuss these operations. Moreover, it is more common to see community-involved efforts aimed at police accountability and transparency, without focusing on the manner in which both police and sheriff along with local city and county governments collaborate with ICE. As a result, and as some warn (Langarica 2015), we may find ourselves in a situation where criminal justice reforms, no matter how meager, may not impact foreign-born and those perceived to be foreign-born.

With attacks at the state level through the passage of bills like House Bill 318 (the Protect Workers Act, fall 2015); the proposed House Bill 100 (the Local Government Immigration Compliance Bill, summer 2016), which was defeated; and bills included in the introduction, it is more important than ever to identify intergovernmental agreements. Community members in particular believe that these state bills protect the communication and functions of the federal 287(g) program, ensuring that any local (city or county) government does not alter its current level of cooperation with ICE.

# CHAPTER 2

# El Hielo anda suelto por esas calles
# (ICE Is Loose in the Streets)

REDEFINING LOCAL ICE COLLABORATION

On February 2, 2019, in Charlotte, NC, Immigration and Customs Enforcement (ICE) director Sean Gallagher described the "new normal" for ICE enforcement practices throughout North Carolina. The purpose? To deter more communities from challenging local immigration enforcement. He elaborated:

> Every one of our targeted arrests, is consistent with the type of enforcement activity that occurs in the state on a daily basis as well as across the country. . . . The advocates and some of the press would like you to believe that we indiscriminately arrest individuals in the community and again it's this type of rhetoric that has a chilling effect. . . . It also shows that we conduct this specific, targeted enforcement—going after specific individuals at specific places. . . . The uptick you've seen—again—is a direct result of some of the dangerous policies that some of our county sheriffs have put in place and it really forces my officers to go out on the street to conduct more enforcement operations out in the community, at court houses, at residences, during traffic stops—this is a direct correlation between the Sheriffs dangerous policies of not cooperating with ICE and the fact that we still have to execute our important law enforcement mission.

What Gallagher did not mention were the various ways ICE continues to operate behind closed doors and the various maneuvers (both public and private) that crimmigration entities may engage in, both during blatantly aggressive enforcement periods and during "normal" enforcement periods.[1] In both instances, local law enforcement and ICE officials engage in a form of racialized social control to reach their goals. This chapter focuses on the persistent nature of this racialized social control while also highlighting all the ways this persistence occurs. This chapter also explains how local immigration enforcement persists in multiple ways through law enforcement, sometimes reinforced by additional government agencies. Sometimes this occurs in overt ways (like 287[g] programs), yet more often it happens through covert practices, such as standard operating protocols and procedures and financial exchanges occurring well beyond the moment of an immigrant's arrest. Furthermore, this chapter builds on previous research by focusing on often overlooked criminal-legal agencies within the larger prison industrial complex capable of collaborating and communicating with ICE. Throughout this chapter, I refer to these avenues of collaboration and communication as the *poli-migra* (*poli* meaning multiple in Spanish, and *migra* meaning ICE), touch points (according to ICE), or the many tentacles of ICE.

Immediately after the 2016 presidential election, community members across the country sought reassurance from local government agencies regarding immigration enforcement practices that were outlined most notably in two executive orders: Border Security and Immigration Enforcement Improvements, and Enhancing Public Safety in the Interior of the United States.[2] These executive orders, among many things, broadened the categories for enforcement, pushed for more ICE and Customs and Border Patrols agents, encouraged more 287(g) programs along the border, put more emphasis on the construction and funding of a border wall, and expanded expedited removal. While some local government agencies stated they would not engage in harsher enforcement, they did little to engage in greater transparency regarding the normalized way they *did* engage in enforcement. Unfortunately, these responses from local government and local law enforcement in particular do not delve into the complexities of communication, collaboration, and financial exchanges with ICE and Department of Homeland Security entities, which occurred and continue to occur regardless of the change in presidential administrations.

Scholars and community members alike tend to focus on the question of whether local law enforcement is "going to round up immigrants." Yet this focus distracts from a much more complicated process that transcends local policies while simultaneously highlighting the local-level decision-making capabilities detailed in chapters 2–5. Furthermore, it is unclear whether those local-level decision makers, namely city and county leadership, recognize their ability to implement or refuse to implement immigration enforcement. For example, county leadership could recommend law enforcement not engage in immigration enforcement and could push for more transparency from local law enforcement in this arena. One thing is certain: they do have the ability to involve non-white communities in their governing processes.

Community-based initiatives like the Faith Action Identification Program and Building Integrated Communities are creating opportunities for local law enforcement agencies to become involved in immigrant and Latinx communities in North Carolina, yet these relationships could also allow for much deeper conversations about the role of local law enforcement with ICE. The Faith Action ID program began in 2014 in Greensboro, North Carolina, as a way "to build greater understanding, trust and cooperation between local law enforcement and other local sectors and our diverse community" by providing a community identification for those unable to obtain a state-issued identification (Faith Action International House 2022).[3] One key component of the program and identification-issuing process is the requirement for card holders—mostly immigrants—to attend an orientation with local law enforcement. Building Integrated Communities (BIC) is described on their website as, "a community planning and leadership initiative that partners with North Carolina local governments to create inclusive practices and policies for residents born in other countries. Local governments and community stakeholders work together to improve communication, public safety, mobility, entrepreneurship, and leadership of immigrant and refugee residents" (Building Integrated Communities 2022).

These efforts also serve the twofold purpose of providing one of the only opportunities for local law enforcement to proactively communicate with the Latinx immigrant community and of allowing the community to obtain information about collaboration, communication, and financial exchanges between local law enforcement and ICE—since various requests to ICE from national organizations for similar information have been unsuccessful.

When local law enforcement agencies and local governing bodies choose to focus their attention on the most intrusive aspects of immigration enforcement, they limit their public presentation of their involvement. More intentional conversations about collaboration could include the additional dimensions proposed in this chapter (immigrant arrest procedures, data transparency, funding streams, interagency procedures) to also resolve issues of transparency and accountability, particularly if the goals of a "receiving" community are to become more welcoming, a goal that many of these local governing bodies have stated by adopting various resolutions with no real policy changes.

As highlighted throughout this book, local sheriffs and police chiefs make the ultimate decision whether to enter into specific agreements with ICE and other entities. State-level agreements occur with little publicity. Yet this state level is only one dimension of immigration enforcement, neglecting other mechanisms, such as the technology- and data-sharing capabilities characteristic of the former version of the Secure Communities program (Pedroza 2013). Secure Communities mainly served to create a database-sharing tool

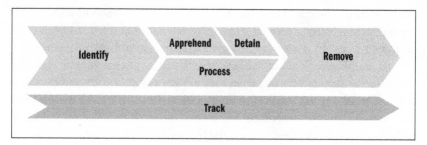

Figure 2.1. Criminal alien enforcement lifecycle (ICE 2019).

between ICE and local law enforcement once a person reached a jail facility. This tool was paired with a set of deportation priorities, which then changed in 2014 to become the Priority Enforcement Program (PEP) until Secure Communities was reintroduced through an Executive Order in 2017 (fig. 2.1).

According to ICE training material for a Secure Communities crash course, the initiative would allow for greater identification capabilities within various aspects of the criminal justice system also known as ICE "touch points."

North Carolina may be unique in the number of 287(g) programs throughout the country, but it is not unique when it comes to other forms of communication, collaboration, and financial exchanges with ICE. Take California, for example—a state considered the beacon of progressive immigration policies, which eventually passed the CA Trust Act (2014), CA Values Act (2017), and the CA Truth Act (2017) (ICE Out of California 2022). The Trust Act set a standard to limit ICE requests to local jails to hold immigrants for extra time while ICE decided whether to pick them up. The Values Act limited local resources being used for immigration enforcement purposes and created "safe spaces" for immigrants in a variety of settings. The Truth Act provides Know Your Rights information to immigrants prior to ICE interviews, notifies them of ICE notifications, and requires local bodies to hold community forums regarding ICE operations. Why the need for so many? Because immigration enforcement partnerships are complex, with limited oversight mechanisms built in. The organizers and activists that pushed for these series of acts refer to this complexity as the *pulpo-migra* (fig. 2.2), where various programs represent a unique tentacle of ICE operations (NDLON 2016).[4]

On the other hand, both local law enforcement and local governments may attempt to provide support for the integration of immigrant, predominantly Latinx communities, but participation with ICE may ultimately be a deterrent for such efforts (Marrow 2009). Yet scholars who write about immigrant inclusion policies (Williams 2015) and the politics of reception (Fussell 2014) have

Figure 2.2. El Pulpo-Migra. Courtesy of Claudia Bautista.

not thoroughly defined the ways in which local law enforcement and governments play a role in the collaboration, communication, and other exchanges
with ICE. This raises the question whether communities are comfortable
with partial policies labeled as welcoming or whether—provided with all the
information about collaboration, communication, and financial exchanges—
communities are willing to live with a patchwork of policies (Varsanyi, Lewis,
Provine, and Decker 2012). Drawing on various conversations with lawyers,
community activists, and law enforcement with additional context gathered
from administrative records, this chapter aims to expand our understanding
of local collaboration with ICE by focusing on the federal, state, and local decisions that agencies can make. As this chapter demonstrates, additional ICE
collaboration occurs at the local and state levels—in all arenas of the prison
industrial complex (e.g., adult corrections, probation, courts, etc.). Although
these are often partnerships dictated by a federal agency, buy-in may come
from both state and local government agencies. By understanding these complexities, we—like many of the community members in future chapters—can
start to interrogate these policies in our own communities.

Menjívar and Abrego (2012b) also highlight the impact of legal violence in
three localized areas—family, workplace, and schools—which ultimately negatively impacts immigrant incorporation. They conclude with policy recommendations, including having "strong worker protections, and go[ing] after
employers that exploit immigrant workers" and that "the government should
also ensure that schools are safe places, free of Immigration and Customs

Enforcement intrusion" (38). These recommendations place responsibility on a variety of bureaucracies. Other researchers previously focused their attention surveying police and sheriffs to ask under what circumstances "officers would check immigration status and/or report to ICE" (Provine, Varsanyi, Lewis, and Decker 2016, 67). More recent surveys did not include information from sheriffs (Fisher Williamson 2018).

In line with this research meant to pinpoint sites of collaboration, cooperation, and communication, this chapter explains how local immigration enforcement by law enforcement and additional government agencies persists in varying degrees. Sometimes this occurs in overt (like 287[g] programs), yet more often it happens through covert practices, such as standard operating protocols and procedures and financial exchanges occurring well beyond the moment of an immigrant's arrest. This also updates previous research, which laid out some of these practices during 2007–10 (Provine, Varsanyi, Lewis, and Decker 2016). Furthermore, this chapter expands previous research by including other agencies within the larger prison industrial complex capable of collaborating and communicating with ICE.

## Policing Immigrants at the Federal Level

In *Policing Immigrants: Local Law Enforcement on the Front Lines* (2016), Provine, Varsanyi, Lewis, and Decker describe the 287(g) program and the beginning of Secure Communities as key components of the devolution of local immigration enforcement practices. They also survey police chiefs and sheriffs, asking whether these officials and their corresponding departments were engaged in specific ICE collaboration efforts like 287(g) program MOUs, 287(g) jail MOUs, ICE officers embedded in department, and no ICE participation/assistance. They investigated also whether the agency had a written policy regarding interactions with immigrants, or whether officers were provided with training for interactions with undocumented immigrants (Provine, Varsanyi, Lewis, and Decker 2016, 48). Their extensive coverage of Secure Communities, the 287(g) program, and survey responses begin to provide a glimpse of the various agreements of cooperation, rightly termed the "multilayered jurisdictional patchwork" (Varsanyi, Lewis, Provine, and Decker 2012). ICE refers to these as an "umbrella of services and programs" (ICE 2008).

The Secure Communities Program is one of the more notable components of the ICE ACCESS umbrella of available programs. Others include the Criminal Alien Program (CAP); Law Enforcement Support Centers (LESC); and operations focused on smuggling (Operation Firewall), violent gang activity (Operation Community Shield), and asset forfeiture.

Although local law enforcement never spoke extensively about the distinctions between the various collaborative efforts with ICE, ICE agents were very careful not to discuss another partnership or collaborative effort when answering questions about the 287(g) program. A 287(g) steering committee meeting held on April 20, 2017 at the Henderson County Detention Center illustrates this careful maneuvering:

> Well most jails m'am, what they do is fingerprint every individual whether they're a United States citizen or not—they get fingerprinted. Those fingerprints then go into a database that informs us or the FBI whether they want them out of the country or not. That's how that takes place.
>
> The fingerprints are being read by command centers across the country. The difference between that and the 287(g) program is that the 287(g) program is on site encountering them, processing them and assisting. They're a force multiplier to identifying people and initiating the encounter.
>
> Sir, real quick we're addressing this in a lot of jurisdictions right now. What we're here for today is to talk about the 287(g) program—it is completely separate from the detainer point that you brought up. The 287(g) program identifies someone at intake as to whether or not they are in this country illegally, notifies ICE that they are in this country illegally and from there they either contact us and let us know and we either come pick them up or they get adjudicated throughout [the process].

In similar incidents in the Mecklenburg County 287(g) Steering Committee meetings in December 2015 and 2016, community members requested information about the program's budget, which also required ICE to make distinctions about revenue from the various programs they implement at the local level. For community members, they began to understand that they were being fed limited information and that the issue of ICE collaboration was more complex than expected.

The 2018 sheriff elections forced ICE to make distinctions among its programs, particularly in localities where candidates included noncompliance with ICE as part of their platform. Unfortunately, ICE officials also took this opportunity to further threaten and demonize the Latinx community by saying that more raids would occur. This is characteristic of four recent responses by ICE officials—mainly from the southeast communications director Bryan Cox—justifying an increase in local ICE raids if these localities ended local partnerships and communication with ICE. These threats were put into action throughout the state, beginning in March 2018 in western North Carolina, which experienced increased ICE arrests prior to Henderson County's annual 287(g) steering committee meeting.

Community members with local organization Companeros Inmigrantes de las Montanas en Accion (CIMA) followed ICE around western North Carolina for three days during these arrests and then turned their attention to encouraging community members to show up to the annual steering committee meeting in an effort to question ICE about the recent raids. During that steering committee meeting, ICE officials made it clear that ending the 287(g) program in that county would increase the likelihood of more arrests by ICE officials out in the community. Moreover, they emphasized the possibility of "collateral" arrests, whereby community members were subject to arrests even if they were not on a specific list but were "encountered" by ICE officials out in the field (DeGrave 2018; Feldblum 2018).

In addition to such measures, other joint task forces and interagency collaboration with ICE may also occur; often they can instill fear into communities because of the inability to differentiate which agency is ultimately "rounding up immigrants." For example, in 2017, in Durham, North Carolina—a place thought to be one of the safest places for immigrants—ICE participated in a U.S. Marshals Joint Fugitive Task Force (Willets 2017a). This confusion about which agency is in fact going door to door looking for people is further complicated when ICE officials wear clothes with police logos. Earlier that same year, a bill was introduced by congressional representative Nydia Velazquez, a Democrat from New York, that would prohibit ICE officers from wearing pieces of clothing with "police" printed on it (M. Green 2017). This concern also arose in questions from various community members in public forums, who questioned whether they could call local law enforcement if someone, perhaps ICE, came to their door but were not recognizable as local law enforcement officers. Some agencies stated that would be fine and then attempted to explain what documents ICE would need for the local agency to be limited in their actions.

Many of the local law enforcement agencies spoke about the courtesy call they would get when ICE was in the area, although they simultaneously denied any participation in such "surprise" operations. In addition, local law enforcement officers reiterated that they would help in cases when ICE was clearly going after a criminal, as the removal of such a person would benefit all communities, both immigration and citizen alike. However, it is unclear in what circumstances many of the local law enforcement agencies would participate in other areas. That is why it is necessary and illuminating to explore the context and conditions needed for local law enforcement to aid ICE when channels of communication and collaboration are not present. Furthermore, sporadic ICE raids highlight and complicate the role of local law enforcement and local government entities when ICE may be searching for specific individuals in schools, churches, and the like (Durkie 2017), even though these locations are considered "sensitive locations," according to ICE (October 24, 2011, memo).

Increasingly, local law enforcement agencies are present in K–12 public schools as school resource officers (SROs), shifting the context of interaction for immigrant youth. Since ICE labels these locations as "sensitive," there is little attention paid to a school's role in immigration matters. This changed in 2016 in North Carolina and across the country in response to the NC6—six young immigrants arrested by ICE in North Carolina, one as he left his house to wait for the school bus—forcing some community groups to push for sanctuary policies within the public school system. Such policies limit school information sharing with ICE and make any information sharing harder by routing requests up to the school district's superintendent. Efforts such as these in Durham and Wake Counties might also provide a renewed interested in limiting information sharing not only with ICE but also with local law enforcement.

## Policing Immigrants at the State Level

In 2017, at least thirty-six states and Washington, D.C., considered legislation regarding sanctuary policies or noncompliance with ICE (Morse, Polkey, Deatherage, and Ibarra 2019), and proposals in thirty-three states would prohibit this. Variations exist to stop collaboration and to implement restrictive state-level legislation. As of 2019, thirty states had pending legislation related to sanctuary or noncompliance with ICE detainers while twenty-one states also proposed opposite or prohibitory legislation (NCSL 2019). With regard to immigration, the National Conference of State Legislators labels states as prosanctuary, antisanctuary, and no position. Unfortunately, this categorization fails to include the biometric screening infrastructure first implemented in the days of Secure Communities, a program that facilitates the data sharing with ICE of almost every jail in the country, which often goes overlooked in research and at the National Conference of State Legislators. Although previous research conducted in 2009–10 showed that 25 percent of surveyed sheriff's offices did not participate with ICE, by 2013, this grew to 100 percent participation or assistance (Provine, Varsanyi, Lewis, and Decker 2016). The implementation of Secure Communities throughout the country provides data sharing every time someone is booked into a jail, meaning that sheriffs cannot opt out of this type of participation and assistance. More specifically, the Immigrant Legal Resource Center in their online local enforcement map outlines at least seven voluntary decisions that sheriffs alone can make regarding ICE collaboration such as asking about immigration status, operating with a 287(g) program, having an ICE detention contract, among others. Some states also have specific legislation related to particular ICE partnerships. As of September 2019, two states, Illinois and California, had passed statewide bans against implementing a 287(g) program, and three states had a 287(g) partnership housed in the Department of Corrections (Nichanian 2019).

First introduced in 2008 and implemented throughout the country, county by county, by 2013, the Secure Communities biometric data-sharing tool allowed for a suspected undocumented person's prints to be run through the ICE database (IDENT) along with other federal and state databases, like state bureaus of investigation, state identification bureaus, and the Federal Bureau of Investigation. Unlike other communication practices, state-level policy approved this tool and form of digital communication, most often with the state identification bureaus. Although the first iteration of Secure Communities officially ended when the Priority Enforcement Program was introduced during the Obama administration under Department of Homeland Security secretary Jeh Johnson, the data sharing did not end, meaning that this component continued under the PEP. At first, it was unclear how the second iteration of Secure Communities, implemented through the Public Safety in the Interior of the United States Executive Order issued by the Trump administration, differs from the first iteration of the program or if the data sharing will continue as before.

At the state level, less scrutiny exists for state-level immigration enforcement partnerships. One such area is in adult corrections. In 2007, the *Raleigh News and Observer* highlighted the relationships between ICE and the state prison system. In that coverage, it was reported that the North Carolina Division of Prisons even had a special position, led by Mary Lou Rogers, to oversee the ICE program, which consisted of officers making weekly visits to state prisons to pick up immigrants. At that time, fifty-seven prisoners per month entered into deportation proceedings (Collins 2007). It appears this office no longer exists (since 2008) in public documents and reporting, and it is unclear what is still occurring in this arena except anecdotally.

According to the State Criminal Alien Assistance Program (SCAAP) award information administered by the Bureau of Justice Assistance (BJA) and meant to partially reimburse the cost of holding undocumented immigrants in local or state facilities, 2017 awards to the state of North Carolina totaled $2,016,406.00. Since 2008, the BJA has awarded $33,119,489.00 to the state. For that same year, forty-six states (seven of which were solely reimbursed to the state department of corrections or a similar office), Puerto Rico, Guam, the Commonwealth of the Northern Mariana Islands, and American Samoa also received awards. North Carolina state budget documentation does not include much else regarding this form of revenue. From 2008 to 2016, this amount was requested for 17,877 unique individuals, a little more than the estimated number of immigrants deported through Mecklenburg County sheriff's 287(g) program during the same time. Since 2016, there has been a slight increase in this reimbursement avenue. Although a specific office no longer exists, funding streams do not lie and instead tell us that immigrants are being turned over to ICE at a "touch point" in the adult corrections systems.

But that's just only one of those "touch points" in the system. Probation is another. This information mainly describes financial exchanges through the Department of Public Safety's Adult Corrections Division. Under that division is Community Corrections, also known as Probation and Post Release Supervision and Parole. According to *Policy and Procedures of the North Carolina Department of Public Safety Division of Adult Correction and Juvenile Justice Community Corrections* (Chapter C: Offender Supervision Section .0624 UN-DOCUMENTED IMMIGRANTS AND DEPORTATION), "Community Corrections has a partnership with Immigration Customs and Enforcement (ICE) that will assist officers with the identification and possible removal of undocumented or illegal immigrants placed on probation/parole." In a 2016 policy and procedures manual (NCDPS 2016), this pertains to "offender notifications," special initiatives, case management, "offenders not yet deported," and "offenders deported." While this information is kept hidden, it shows a specific policy was created for interactions with immigrants in probation and parole supervision.

Community members across the state continue to report that members of their communities are being picked up by ICE when they arrive at their probation check-in meetings, namely in Buncombe, Mecklenburg, and Durham Counties. These counties recently moved to limit their cooperation within the jails by getting rid of their 287(g) agreements and by limiting ICE detainer requests to hold immigrants until ICE decides whether to pick them up. Although, these postconviction collaborative efforts with ICE may not be new, they require our attention as communities continue to push back against local jail partnerships and the threat of collateral arrests.

## Policing Immigrants at the Local Level

Local law enforcement and local government officials—particularly in the Triad (High Point, Winston-Salem, Greensboro) and the Triangle (Raleigh, Durham, Chapel Hill) areas of North Carolina—respond to community concerns about immigration enforcement by making the general statement "We are not ICE." They may not be ICE agents or have all the authority of ICE, but they may collaborate, correspond, and participate in financial exchanges with the agency. Certain agencies attempted to explain the process by which a person could encounter ICE after a traffic stop or other encounter with local law enforcement. Most agencies were not forthcoming to community members in steering committee meetings and public meetings about all the ways in which they collaborate, correspond, or make financial exchanges with ICE. Furthermore, when the process is explained, local law often enforcement reiterates their commitment to keeping everyone safe—both citizens and undocumented people—by justifying their hypothetical support for efforts to capture criminals who may be undocumented.

This was during the run-up to the 2016 election, yet the statements remained the same even after the announcement of the two executive orders related to immigration enforcement during the Trump administration. These orders, the Border Security and Immigration Enforcement Improvements order and Enhancing Public Safety in the Interior of the United States order, encouraged more local participation with ICE. In conversations with local law enforcement both before and after these executive orders, agencies typically did not discuss their role in the dimensions of enforcement. Although many of these dimensions (immigrant arrest procedures, data and identification transparency, funding streams, interagency procedures) are applicable only within the county jail and through the sheriff's office, police agencies and local government officials play key roles in the several ways.

## LOCAL GOVERNMENTS

Local decision makers may or may not recognize their involvement in these dimensions, yet they still maintain some influence over the local law enforcement agencies, particularly regarding fiscal oversight. For example, the city council must pass police department budgets, and the county commissioners must pass the budget for the sheriff. The most obvious instance of this type of oversight exists in counties where the sheriff's office presented their plan to implement a 287(g) program with ICE, making requests for additional funding from the county commissioners to hire new staff, build new facilities, and more. Because county commissioners and the individual sheriff's offices are not required to sign individual agreements for programs like Secure Communities, there seems to be confusion and little understanding of their role in implementing programs signed into law by a state governing body. This is also the case when navigating state-level legislation, which is attempting to preempt the ways cooperation and collaboration occurs with ICE, through bills like Senate Bill 4 in Texas, and House Bill 318 in North Carolina. Texas Senate Bill 4 forces law enforcement agencies to comply with ICE detainers, punishes local governments that do not enforce immigration laws, and bans any limits on ICE enforcement. North Carolina House Bill 318 prohibited local governments from limiting immigration enforcement, expanded the use of E-Verity, and limited the use of non-state-issued identification.

Obviously, 287(g) programs, especially the model describe in this book, must be approved by county governments. The five programs in North Carolina were all presented to the county board of commissioners between 2006 and 2008, yet no consistent financial or detainee information was presented to the county commissioners in public formats over the next ten years. Furthermore, many county commissioners and city council officials have little knowledge of these processes, meaning that they are unable to make educated decisions about ICE cooperation, collaboration, or financial exchanges. What is clear, though, is their unwavering faith in the decision-making capability of the local law enforcement agencies they work with. Across the country, only a handful of local government bodies have encouraged the end to certain partnerships with ICE. In these instances, this stance has come about only through community pressure like that exhibited in 2017 in Harris County, Texas, where community groups like the American Civil Liberties Union (ACLU) of Texas, United We Dream, the Immigrant Legal Resource Center, and the Texas Organizing Project brought awareness to the problems of the 287(g) program. Although an end to the 287(g) program in Harris County did not mean an end to ICE collaboration and communication (Pinkerton and Barned-Smith 2017). The organizers went after one local program, and the response from the state legislator was strong, sending messages to others across the country that localized efforts were powerful enough to cause a preemptive negative statewide response. Ensuring preemption does not occur means tackling ICE collaboration at the state level.

## LAW ENFORCEMENT ENTITIES

### Police Departments

Signed into law by then North Carolina governor Mike Easley, the 2006 Technical Corrections Act reinstated the requirement that anyone applying for a driver's license must provide a valid social security number, eliminating the ability to use an ITIN, or individual taxpayer identification number (Denning Riggsbee 2009). Across the country, each state has the ability to do the same and place limitations on who is eligible to obtain a driver's license or valid form of identification. The Technical Corrections Act effectively meant that, in North Carolina, undocumented people would no longer be able to obtain or renew a driver's license and might therefore end up driving with expired licenses, since no feasible alternative was proposed for these individuals.[5]

Because they also serve the purpose of verifying one's identity, driver's licenses are particularly important when interacting with local law enforcement. Without such a document, local law enforcement often, depending on the agency's procedures and policies, use their discretion and take motorists to the jail facility to attempt to verify their identity. This verification process exposes individuals to a variety of biometric sharing tools, which may begin the process of communicating with ICE. Some local law enforcement agencies across the country recognize this conundrum and choose to participate in initiatives that provide an alternative method for identification, like municipal or organizational IDs. In response to the creation of some of these alternative identifications, state law makers scrutinize their validity and security.[6]

In 2015, the City of Durham Police Department operated with a 287(g) program, until public pressure ended it. Although the program officially ended, an agreement with Homeland Security Investigations (HSI) remained—often used to investigate employees with false work documentation. Their charge is to investigate a variety of criminal activity that may transverse borders, such as financial crimes, cybercrimes, narcotics, and gang activity. HSI also conducts counterterrorism investigations (Oliver 2007). This agreement differs from the 287(g) program, and the Durham police chief maintained that such a collaboration is useful for human and drug trafficking matters (Chen 2015), given that the MOU between the two authorizes a customs agent to be on staff. These task forces or interagency collaboration are rare at the city police department level, and as a result, community members typically focus on the issue of checkpoints or general traffic stops conducted by the local law enforcement agency.

In March 2017, the City of Durham police chief took a bold step to reassure community members at a forum by stating that "checkpoints in the city of Durham have been directed to cease and desist" (Hellerstein 2017). Then chief C. J. Davis clarified her rationale in a press release: "This was done to dispel fears that have currently arisen and to further encourage sustainable relationships with the diverse community we serve." Also present at this forum were representatives from the city and county governing bodies, the superintendent of Durham public schools, and Major Martin from the sheriff's office. Many of the approximately 1,000 people in attendance were there to hear news from the local law enforcement agencies regarding expected implementation of and compliance with the Trump administration's executive orders.

The concerns about traffic stops were not unique to the police department or to Durham. Other reassurance forums including the one in Burlington, North Carolina, where then chief Jeffrey Smythe of the Burlington Police Department brought an enlarged map showing all the checkpoints in his jurisdiction in order to reassure community members that checkpoints were random and not targeted at Latinx communities. Although Chief Smythe and others refuted the notion that racial profiling may be occurring in this type of enforcement practice, much of the community concern stems from the poststop activities—the citations or arrests that can result from driving without a license. Across the various police departments and sheriff's offices, law enforcement expressed the complications they face when stopping someone who is driving without a license. Most made it clear that they may be forced to take someone to jail in order to verify their identity if that person does not have any form of identification.

As an alternative to arresting individuals and verifying their identity at the local jail, some local law enforcement agencies in North Carolina are able to use an organizational ID called the Faith Action Network Identification as a verified form of identification. A program of the Faith Action International House, a nonprofit based in Greensboro, North Carolina, the Faith Action ID cards are available to any resident who may have limited access to government-issued forms of ID. They provide ID cards to those with a verifiable form of identification acceptable by certain law enforcement agencies, health centers, and businesses. Participants must attend a mandatory orientation at a monthly ID drive and provide proof of photo ID and address. These orientations became an even more important piece of my research once the new Trump administration began, serving as a mechanism for nonprofit partners to utilize the relationships developed in the Faith Action ID drives as an entryway to discussing immigration enforcement at the local level.

Such a program is characteristic of the "welcomeness" dynamic (also known as immigrant integration efforts), which is an attempt by local law enforcement to create more positive engagement with immigrant communities (Fisher Williamson 2018). As of the spring of 2017, approximately 10,000 identifications had been issued through the participation of four sheriff's offices, fifteen police departments, and four health centers. Similar issues with identification were also expressed by local law enforcement agencies in western North Carolina, where the Faith Action ID program is not implemented, except in one location, as of 2022. In this regard, community members may feel more comfortable reaching out to local law enforcement with concerns about national- and state-level changes.

In addition, local law enforcement benefits from the ID program by receiving positive publicity for interacting with a minority community, by encouraging individuals to report more crimes, and by taking these opportunities to recruit bilingual individuals. As Burlington's police chief, Jeffrey Smythe, put it, "The Burlington Police Department has been involved with the Faith Action ID Card program for several years. Every month we are able to attend an ID drive and engage new residents. We discuss many aspects of public safety and build great relationships with folks who previously were suspicious or fearful of the police. These relationships lead to enhanced safety for immigrants and citizens alike" (Faith Action ID Impact Document 2017). According to Mike Richey, deputy chief of the Greensboro Police Department, "The FAITH ID program has helped the Greensboro Police Department reach out, get to know, and develop trust in a section of our community that has been traditionally underserved and over victimized. The bridges built in trust through this partnership have led to a safer community overall, not just for the ID recipients." (FaithAction International House 2017)

### Sheriff's Offices

The trend for many municipal police is to take a community policing approach, but sheriff's offices have other responsibilities beyond their city counterparts. Most of this book focuses on the role sheriffs play in local immigration enforcement policies, whether in deciding protocols for interacting with immigrants, administering data sharing with additional government agencies, making decisions to hold immigrants after criminal charges, or monitoring court proceedings, among other responsibilities. This section reviews more in depth the administrative policies they control, including additional intergovernmental agreements beyond the 287(g) program, jail administrative duties, and financial exchanges. These are important aspects of sheriff responsibilities because for the most part, they are voluntary, meaning that sheriffs have the autonomy to make decisions that can impact any immigrant they come in contact with.

Although some local law enforcement agencies may make financial exchanges with ICE through reimbursement structures, some county jails also rent space to ICE. Intergovernmental service agreements are agreements between the federal government—more specifically ICE—and a state or local government to provide detention beds in jails, prisons, and other local or government detention facilities. While government-owned, local, state, or private agencies may provide the detention services, some of these facilities may even be dedicated for federal use, in an intergovernmental support agreement (IGSA). Although IGSAs were less common throughout the state, particularly outside of counties with a 287(g) program, in 2015, New Hanover County Detention Center and Forsyth County Jail both had an agreement. Beyond the agreements made with fully functioning county detention centers, there is evidence that in some counties, Mecklenburg for example, the prospect of ICE renting space in a newly constructed county facility was discussed beginning in 2007, prior to the construction of the detention center. In an August 14, 2007, detention update to the Mecklenburg County Board of Commissioners, the county manager and sheriff provided some of the following highlights: "ICE funds are only available for renting space. They do not have upfront funds to contribute towards building a facility, ICE is interested in renting bed space if the County builds a new facility" (Mecklenburg County BOC 2007). Furthermore, it was suggested that the agreement would even generate revenue for the county and that "the facility would house immigrants apprehended from the Mid-Atlantic and Southeast regions and not just in North Carolina." This last point further illustrates the hub-and-spoke model previously mentioned, where one facility aids surrounding counties. U.S. marshals can also request rental space to house federal detainees, both citizens and undocumented persons. Guilford County, Mecklenburg County, and Wake County facilities also serve as holding spaces for U.S. marshal districts.

Sheriffs are also jail administrators, responsible for booking processes after someone is arrested. In North Carolina, biometric data-sharing technology associated with Secure Community was implemented between November 12, 2008, and March 15, 2011, with the Wake County Sheriff's Office being the first to adopt (ICE-SC activated 2013). The memorandum of agreement (MOA) between ICE and the North Carolina State Bureau of Investigation was made official in November 2009, meaning that some county jails were early adopters of the program prior to the statewide agreement (North Carolina State Bureau of Investigation 2009). Included in this MOA was a list of three offense categories: level 1, major drug offenses, national security crimes, and violent crimes; level 2, minor drug and property offenses; and level 3, other offenses (2). These categories later changed in 2014 under the Obama administration and the implementation of the PEP. The PEP outlined three priority levels, too, but reduced the scope of what was prioritized. Priority 1 included those representing threats to national security, border security, and public safety; priority 2, those accused of misdemeanors, and new immigration violators; and priority 3, other immigration violators (U.S. Department of Homeland Security 2014).

In the fall of 2016, information provided through public records requests to the Durham County Sheriff's Office did not include information regarding the county's participation with ICE; instead, the documents noted that there is no formal policy with ICE. Furthermore, they maintained, "in the absence of a formal agreement, the Sheriff's Office complies with state and federal law. . . . There are no internal or external communications related to the PEP, Secure Communities (S-COMM) during the timeframe you've requested. . . . Because the Sheriff's Office does not participate in PEP or S-COMM programs, we do not maintain individual records related to PEP or S-COMM."[7]

Yet, in subsequent 2017 public forums through the Faith Action Identification orientations, the Durham County Sheriff Office representatives stated they were involved in Secure Communities. And two more opportunities to clarify sheriff cooperation with ICE left some doubt about operations. Information presented to the City of Durham Human Relations Commission included a memo from the Durham County sheriff stating that they did in fact participate in Secure Communities (Willets 2017b). In the fall of 2017 a major with the sheriff's office then presented contradictory information in a public forum focused on local-level participation with ICE where the sheriff's office, police chief, and city and county officials gave comments about their efforts to curb fears in the immigrant community. Across a period of about six months, administrators gave four different responses about participation in this dimension, causing alarm for some community members and confusion for most. In this instance and similarly in other counties, local officials tried to avoid these questions, perhaps because they might reveal more information about the collaboration but more often than not, some were just blissfully ignorant of the processes and agreements. That is, until they were held accountable.

Each of the five sheriff's offices with a 287(g) program in North Carolina have dedicated personnel who are deputized as immigration officers. During the initial implementation of the programs, some of the sheriff's offices requested additional funding from their respective county board of commissioners to support such activities. Table 2.1 shows the number of trained and active deputized officers for fiscal year 2015 for the sheriff's offices with a 287(g) program. Over the years, the number of trained officers declined, and the 2015 numbers are more of a midpoint look at the program. This information also was presented in steering committee meetings. Mecklenburg and Wake Counties had the greatest number of trained officers over the course of the program.

Those agencies with agreements with HSI, like the City of Durham, also employ dedicated personnel who perform certain immigration enforcement duties. Some of these duties included verifying the immigration status of those booked into the jail.

Once an individual was set to be released, this information would also be exchanged with ICE, and ICE would issue a detainer or an ICE hold. ICE makes detainer or ICE hold requests to local law enforcement agencies to hold an undocumented person beyond that individual's release date. Certain circuit-court rulings have determined that detainers are unconstitutional, but this does not currently apply to North Carolina, although many immigrant rights groups appeal to their local officials with this explanation for ending collaboration (ILRC 2021). ) The Transactional Records Access Clearinghouse (TRAC) reports detailed analysis of case-by-case ICE records

Table 2.1. Number of trained and active deputized officers in fiscal year 2015

| County | Trained | Active |
|--------|---------|--------|
| Henderson | 18 | 6 |
| Cabarrus | 14 | 3 |
| Gaston | 20 | 6 |
| Mecklenburg | 29 | 8 |
| Wake | 37 | 17 |

(TRAC n.d.-a). This clearinghouse contains individual records on each recorded detainer or notice request prepared by ICE. Each detainer typically includes information on the law enforcement agency that sent the request, as well as information about the individual who was the subject of the request. In addition to demographic information, individual's detailed criminal histories are also included when provided.

Unfortunately, this database is becoming less reliable, something TRAC has noted, but alternative methods of tracking down this information are limited. During the Trump administration, we even saw ICE's failed attempt to publicly shame a law enforcement agency that may have denied detainer requests because they did not have up-to-date information (T. Vasquez 2017). TRAC was established in 1989 as a research center jointly sponsored by the S. I. Newhouse School of Public Communications and the Martin J. Whitman School of Management at Syracuse University with the purpose to provide the American people—and institutions of oversight such as Congress, news organizations, public interest groups, businesses, scholars, and lawyers—with comprehensive information about staffing, spending, and enforcement activities of the federal government. Responses from Freedom of Information Act (FOIA) requests led TRAC to issue the following statement on March 21, 2017:

The agency [Immigration and Customs Enforcement (ICE)] has started withholding other more comprehensive information that ICE previously released to TRAC in response to Freedom of Information Act (FOIA) requests. ICE does not claim the withheld information is exempt from disclosure, it simply claims past releases were discretionary and it is no longer willing to make many of these details available to the public. Because of these ICE refusals, TRAC is unable to update its online free web query tools that allow the public to view ICE activities under both the previous Bush and Obama Administrations. We are also currently in court on another FOIA action trying to obtain ICE records on what fields of information the agency's databases actually track. Even though ICE released these descriptive documents before, ICE now refuses to provide updated listings describing its data. Our brief in that litigation was filed March 10. (TRAC 2017)

The TRAC team collects information about detainer/hold requests across various years, yet some of that information is incomplete because of reporting inconsistencies across various local law enforcement agencies. Figure 2.3 shows the number of counties where ICE sent detainer/hold requests. Although ICE sends the requests to the local law enforcement agency, that agency may not be willing to comply with the requests and hold that person for additional time. In 2018, Guilford and Forsyth Counties reiterated their policies not to honor these requests unless ICE also had an outstanding criminal arrest warrant or a valid court order, citing Fourth Amendment violations (Green 2017). According to the TRAC database, between 2010 and 2015, a majority of the counties in North Carolina were receiving detainer/hold requests, yet it is unclear how many of these county jails were honoring the requests. In addition, in seven counties, ICE sent requests to multiple facilities.

With the lack of reliable ICE detainer information, funding is typically a little easier to track down. Or at least we expect our local governments to be good stewards of our taxpayer dollars. To some extent, studies that focus on the revenue-generating component of the broader prison industrial complex neglect to consider the ways that intergovernmental service agreements allow ICE to rent space in local, state, and federal facilities (Doty and Whitley 2013). A combination of the BJA, Office of Justice programs, and the U.S. Department of Justice, with the U.S. Department of Homeland Security (DHS) administering the SCAAP awards are some sources of funding for local immigration related costs. States and localities are able to apply for these awards by demonstrating various costs, namely those "incurred correctional officer salary costs for incarcerating undocumented criminal aliens who have at least one felony or two misdemeanor convictions for violations of state or local law, and who are incarcerated for at least 4 consecutive days during the reporting period" (BJA 2012). Payment formulas differed slightly each year, but beginning in 2008 (BJA n.d.), payment formulas are available online.[8] The per diem rate range has spanned from $28.16 in 2011 to a high of $41.26 in 2014. In fiscal year 2015, forty-six counties in North Carolina received some amount of SCAAP awards, while the state government received $1,915,850. In that year, the awards ranged from $14.00 in Person County to Mecklenburg County's highest award at $269,859.00. The number of counties receiving similar awards varies over time, but figure 2.4 indicates that more than half of North Carolina counties—over the course of a time period with reliable data tracking—participated in financial exchanges with the Department

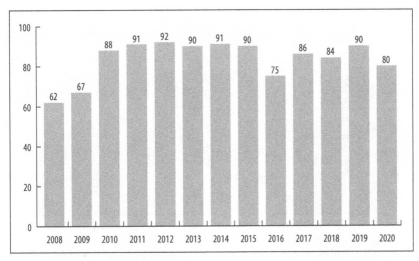

Figure 2.3. Number of North Carolina counties (out of 100) where ICE sent detainer/hold requests, 2008–19 (TRAC n.d.-a).

of Homeland Security, the overarching governing body of ICE. While many people think their county is not involved in ICE collaboration, the number of counties receiving SCAAP awards suggests otherwise. But this information is still limited in painting the whole picture because reimbursements are provided for immigrants with certain offenses and not all immigrants.

Although this is no longer the case, many of the sheriff's offices adopted the 287(g) program introduced the program to their county commissioners with the caveat that it would be fully reimbursed by ICE or the state. For example, meeting minutes summarized then sheriff Rick Davis's rationale for the program in an address at a February 20, 2008, Henderson County meeting,

> Sheriff Davis felt this was an appropriate course of action because of the inability to identify the majority of criminal wanted illegal aliens. . . . An annual loss of an estimated $750,000 to county just from the detention center. . . . It is important for Henderson County to be the "HUB" first and foremost because it would give the Sheriff the discretion as to whether someone that is coming through the detention center with minor crimes would go through the deportation process. This is a relief mechanism to have someone with lower offenses to at least bond out. The majority of the people that are in our Detention Center that are wanted, illegal or not, are there because they were picked up on minor offenses. Persons under arrest will be identified. Henderson County will

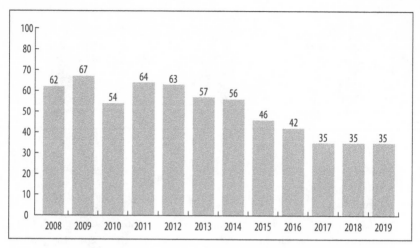

Figure 2.4. Number of North Carolina counties (out of 100) that received SCAAP awards, 2008–20 (BJA, n.d.).

recover all cost then some. . . . Sheriff Davis stated that the Sheriff's Office is fully committed to using only federal money for this plan's operation. (Henderson County BOC 2008a)

The county manager further explained that they would be setting up a separate fund specifically for 287(g) operations from excessive revenue in the county budget: "The Project based on the plan is self-sustaining. It could be based on the projections. Down the road it will be a self-contained Revenue Fund that would basically pay for itself over that period of time." Between 2008 and 2015, the Henderson County Immigration and Customs Fund ranged from $469,151 to $843,908 at its peak in fiscal year 2012–13. Local law enforcement agents have a variety of responsibilities when it comes to interacting with immigrants—some voluntary and some ambiguously followed. These include immigrant arrest procedures, data transparency and identification, funding streams, and interagency procedures. With more than 400 law enforcement agencies in North Carolina, each agency not only has its own way of navigating interactions with immigrants but also has multiple ways to do so. Of course, community members may not recognize all these "touch points," but for immigrants, the uncertainty can make life challenging.

## Conclusion

Initiatives like the Faith Action Identification create opportunities for local law enforcement agencies to become involved in immigrant and Latinx communities in North Carolina, yet these relationships could also allow for much deeper conversations about the role of local law enforcement with ICE. They also serve the twofold purpose of (1) providing one of the only opportunities local law enforcement has to proactively communicate with the Latinx immigrant community and (2) allowing the community to obtain information about collaboration, communication, and financial exchanges between local law enforcement and ICE—since various requests to ICE from national organizations for similar information have been unsuccessful.

Although many see the 287(g) program as the only obvious sign that a local law enforcement agency is communicating with ICE, it is clear from SCAAP award data and detainer information that the communication, collaboration, and financial exchanges occur throughout most of North Carolina. North Carolina may be unique in the number of its 287(g) programs throughout the state, but the state is not unique when it comes to other forms of communication, collaboration, and financial exchanges with ICE.

When local law enforcement agencies and local governing bodies choose to focus their attention only on the most intrusive aspects of immigration enforcement, they limit their public presentation of their involvement. More intentional conversations around dimensions of ICE collaboration would resolve issues of transparency and accountability, particularly if the goal of a receiving community is to become more welcoming—a goal that many of these local governing bodies have stated by adopting various resolutions with no real policy changes. Until then, the following questions remain.

First, would Latinx and immigrant communities cooperate with local law enforcement if those agencies were more forthcoming about their collaboration, correspondence, and financial exchanges with ICE? Local law enforcement encourages the participation of the community, particularly to report crimes occurring within communities that traditionally have a higher police presence, yet it's unclear how communities respond when some "welcoming" policies are in place while these same communities are still fearful of local-level entryways into deportation proceedings. The implementation of the U-Visa program at the local level is another one of the policies—flaunted as a measure of goodwill toward the immigrant community, yet even this program has varying degrees of implementation.

Second, would city councils and county commissioners be willing to interrogate local law enforcement agencies about their practices? What role would progressive politics play in such an effort? Local law enforcement may maintain that they are not "controlled" by elected governing bodies, yet their operating budgets must pass approval. Of course, it is rare to find a city council or county commission that is drastically in opposition to their local law enforcement agencies and willing to interrogate their respective law enforcement agencies about immigration enforcement matters. This becomes more complicated with regard to sheriffs' elected position. However, sheriffs' unique position also means they are subject to political pressure, even though at the national, state, and local levels progressives have not necessarily used this pressure to change the collaboration, communication, and financial exchanges with ICE.

Last, would the public safety arguments made by local law enforcement withstand questions related to ICE collaboration? Local law enforcement, particularly in locations with the Faith Action Identification program, state that the acceptance of the identification card makes it easier for them to complete their job of ensuring public safety and lessens the amount of time and paperwork they need to spend on taking individuals to jail for identification. Priorities for deportation, both previous and current, include threats to public safety and national security threats. These threats may complement or be in opposition to each other, yet it is up to local law enforcement to determine how they will act. Ultimately, local law enforcement and local governing bodies must make decisions about local, state, national, and even international laws while responding to their community-specific needs.

# CHAPTER 3

# The Persistence of 287(g)

"The 287(g) program was originally intended to target and remove undocumented immigrants convicted of violent crimes, human smuggling, gang/organized crime activity, sexual-related offenses, narcotics smuggling and money laundering. However, the program is largely being used to purge towns of any undocumented immigrants, not just those individuals with criminal records, thereby having detrimental effects on North Carolina's communities," said Carolina McCready, a member of the Immigrant Rights Coalition of Henderson County, after a May 4, 2010, event at the historic county courthouse where one hundred community members gathered to support and protest the 287(g) program (Harbin 2010). Although public reactions to this program decreased in subsequent years, the opportunities to engage local crimmigration entities and Immigration and Customs Enforcement (ICE) directly picked back up in 2015, with the addition of 287(g) steering committee meetings across the state. In 2018, sentiments similar to McCready's surfaced in three counties with the 287(g) program. Because of heated sheriff elections in two of those counties—Mecklenburg and Wake Counties—the 287(g) program would eventually end in December 2018, as the new sheriffs took office. However, in Henderson County, the renewal of the program was up for debate, continuing a conversation that also began right before the 2016 sheriff campaign debate described in detail later in this chapter. In this chapter, I begin to answer the question, how do some 287(g) programs persist?

In chapters 1 and 2, I focus on the maintenance of 287(g) practices for the past ten years in North Carolina, an early adopter of local immigration enforcement partnerships like the 287(g) program. Collective efforts challenging the initial implementation of the 287(g) programs were limited in nature, and many local groups did not have the resources to sustain these efforts, especially as they navigated a system not meant for widespread public participation (Prieto 2016) (fig. 3.1).

This chapter focuses on cases where there were minimal challenges to the program, where the political realm did not allow for community participation

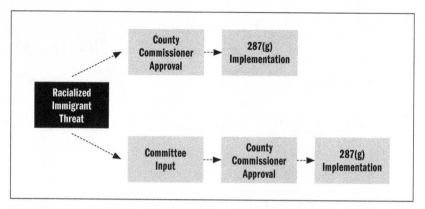

Figure 3.1. 287(g) implementation process.

and subsequent community policing practices, or where initiatives split up community efforts to pressure the sheriff, or any combination of these. In so doing, this chapter both explains the persistence of the 287(g) program in three counties and contributes to a call by Francesca Polletta, author of *Freedom Is an Endless Meeting* (2012), to focus on local movement organizations and leadership, lower-profile efforts to ensure local changes, and the organizational structures that facilitate this (203). In 2023, three of these counties—Henderson, Cabarrus, and Gaston—still operate with 287(g) programs. But two of them—Gaston and Cabarrus—exist with little to no community pushback, perhaps owing to both a smaller immigrant population and the absence of an established immigrant rights center. A review of administrative records shows that community members in Gaston County questioned the intentions of the program, but I was unable to find substantive efforts beyond that point. Surprisingly, the sheriff in Gaston County is also a Democrat, which would further suggest that political affiliation may also not dictate the implementation of local law enforcement partnerships with ICE, in line with recent research in this arena (Thompson 2020).

Program implementation came on the heels of the mass mobilizations of Latinxs in 2006 in response to the Border Protection, Antiterrorism, and Illegal Immigration Control Act of 2005, also known as the Sensenbrenner Bill, and Zepeda-Millán suggests that the decline of that protest wave was the result of an increase in raids, deportations, hate crimes, and state and local anti-immigrant ordinances (2017, 23). At the state level, other campaigns for tuition equity and driver's licenses persist while statewide efforts to limit local deportation practices did not. It is only around 2015 that campaigns, led by some of the central participants in the 2006 protests, have resurfaced to target these local enforcement practices. However, not until 2018 did persistent campaigns targeting sheriff participation—both voluntary and unquestioned practices—in local immigration occur. The sheriffs in the cases studies did not often question the policies and protocols in their jails, instead trusting in those who created them before. These unquestioned practices of adoption, particularly of biometric screening practices, mirror the "rational ignorance" typically used to describe when citizens "do not appear to have concerns intense enough to provoke participation and information gathering" about a particular issue (Robbins, Simonsen, and Feldman 2008).[1] Yet that rational ignorance applies differently to directly impacted individuals (individuals with a precarious legal status) and their predominantly white allies. While white people may operate with this rational ignorance, directly impacted individuals experience a plethora of administrative burdens also known as racialized burdens (Ray, Herd, Moynihan 2020). Administration burden, according to Herd and Moynihan, includes learning costs (collecting information about public services), psychological costs (associated stigmas and frustrations), and compliance costs (material burdens), all of which were exacerbated for the predominately Spanish-speaking immigrants within these communities. According to Victor Ray, Pamela Herd, and Donald Moynihan, racialized burdens on the other hand "are the experience of learning, compliance and psychological costs, which serve as tools to reinforce racial inequality; they are the handmaidens of the racialized state."

The present political climate—characterized by the blatant anti-immigrant rhetoric during the 2016 presidential elections that continues today—has also encouraged local-level resistance against immigration enforcement partnerships. In some ways, this reflects conditions similar to the 2006 Latinx waves of protest that emerged under Republican Party control, strong nativist sentiments after 9/11, and a looming legislative threat in the Sensenbrenner Bill of 2005 (Zepeda-Millán 2017). Furthermore, few national efforts prior to the Trump administration have forced the Democratic Party, both locally and nationally, to take on these concerns, with limited national movement within this two-party political system.

Both researchers and activists are struggling to understand who is responsible in a deportation continuum or regime and in local immigration enforcement more broadly. While many scholars focus on the impacts of 287(g) programs and Secure Communities, seldom do they focus on all entryways into the criminal-legal system. By focusing on only one piece of the puzzle, we limit our understanding of these entities, and we ultimately miss strategic "targets" of social movement organizations hoping to alter this deportation continuum. But this confusion also limits us to those organizations that are participating in the deportation process without broadening the understanding of how this process itself contributes to citizenship and imprisonment more generally or how other civil agencies—particularly elected officials—participate. When they do participate, we should label them crimmigration entities.

## A Sealed-Off Political Realm

Unlike the police chief of a local police department, who may still collaborate with ICE, sheriffs are elected officials with a complicated relationship to a county board that has varying levels of oversight, as described in previous chapters. In most states throughout the United States, the sheriff is the most senior law enforcement officer in the county and is also the head administrator of local jails. Although the county board, who are also elected officials, may direct and advise the sheriff, the sheriff decides many functions without their oversight, like entering into partnerships with ICE or other federal agencies.

Although Democrats as a party are expected to be more progressive than Republicans on certain issues, sheriffs in particular may not fit that description. Nationally, Daniel Thompson (2020) found that in a sample of 3,500 partisan sheriff elections, these sheriffs comply with immigration authorities at nearly the same rate and hold more similar views across party lines than the general public. This recent research expands on similar results from a national survey of 500 elected sheriffs, which indicates that sheriffs' ideology and personal characteristics shape their views of immigrants, resulting in attitudes that play a role in decisions about whether or not to comply with immigration enforcement (Farris and Holman 2017).

Although Abigail Fisher Williamson's research (2018) focuses on police chiefs rather than sheriffs, she expands some of this local research to include views from city and county government officials. Of the five 287(g) programs in North Carolina in 2018, two functioned under a conservative Democrat, and one of them received an award from ICE for ten years of service. While it seems from this research that political party is not a strong determiner in sheriff immigration compliance, in the following chapter, I suggest that partisan elections may matter more if the candidate's race is also considered. At the local level, neither Democrats nor Republicans nor the nonprofits that support them have made substantial progress on immigrant rights in various localities across North Carolina and more broadly in the southeastern United States because of a constrained political climate. South Carolina, Tennessee, Georgia, Alabama, Mississippi, and Florida are all Republican controlled (one political party holds the governorship, a majority of the state senate, and a majority in the state house) and have legislation in place that supports law enforcement's full compliance with ICE. In that regard, there is not much incentive for political parties to take up pro-immigrant legislation and initiatives. Instead, cities and smaller municipalities are experimenting with immigrant integration initiatives in the Southeast. For example, in 2013, the mayor of Atlanta, Georgia, announced the city's participation in Welcoming America's Welcoming Cities and Counties Initiative. The committee formed to implement this initiative made twenty recommendations, and some were immediately implemented, such as formally establishing the mayor's Office of Immigrant Affairs, partnering with the United States Citizenship and Immigration Services (USCIS) to promote citizenship awareness, and partnering with the Atlanta Police Department to launch a multicultural liaison unit (McDaniel 2018). This is just one example of a locality taking its own action while the state legislature is unwilling to budge.

The lack of progress and initiatives to further incorporate or integrate immigrants into localities in North Carolina and the United States may result from issues of rational ignorance but are also tied to the "cozy consensus" among sheriffs and other elected officials, which Kalir and Wissink (2016) note occurs among nonprofits and state actors within negotiations of immigrant belonging and community safety. Kalir and Wissink (2016, 34)— "focusing ethnographically on deportation case managers and NGO workers in the Netherlands"—also argue that a dependency on state agents—local law enforcement—emerges in times of anti-immigrant legislative pushes, which creates a sealed-off political realm. In their case study, Kalir and Wissink (2016) expand on the entities that participate in the deportation process, describing how NGOs and civil society participate in what they call a "deportation continuum."

Most striking are the similarities between the Departure and Repatriation Service (DT&V) agents in the Netherlands and the responses of local sheriff deputies described by Amada Armenta (2015). Armenta (2012; 2015) conducted two years of ethnographic fieldwork with the Davidson County Sheriff's Office and the Nashville Police Department in Tennessee and found that ICE officials tightly regulated the 287(g) partnership between ICE and the sheriff's office. Sheriff personnel, on the other hand, saw themselves as "objective administrators whose primary responsibilities are to identify and process immigrants for removal" (Armenta 2012, 191). Armenta's study highlights the role of one particular crimmigration entity, yet little has surfaced about how this entity works with other such entities, like city and county governments, to usher in intergovernmental agreements between local law enforcement and ICE enforcement meant to deal with the growing Latinx population, considered by some as a "Latino threat" (Chavez 2013). Both studies find a similar phenomenon: allocating the responsibility for deportation elsewhere, which, in the former, "partially relieves case-managers from the (emotional) consequences of their direct actions" (Kalir and Wissink 2016, 41). According to

**4 LAS MONTAÑAS**

LA VOZ INDEPENDIENTE, 4 DE JULIO 2018

# Muy pocos hispanos votaron en Henderson

REDACCIÓN LA VOZ

Si las políticas del Alguacil de Henderson Charles McDonald para colaborar con las autoridades de inmigración del Gobierno federal han creado una polémica en la comunidad hispana del condado, no mostró que era insatisfecha cuando tuvo la oportunidad en mayo.

McDonald perdió su campaña para segundo mandato completo el 8 de mayo ante el reto de Lowell Griffin, quien McDonald había despedido de su oficina en 2014.

Griffin obtuvo 7,343 votos, o 59 por ciento, a los 5,210 de McDonald.

Sin embargo, una análisis de la votación de esos comicios reveló que muy, muy pocos latinos contaron entre los 12,500 votantes que decidieron quién será el alguacil del condado por las próximas cuatro años.

De los 1,303 votantes de Henderson que se identificaron como hispanos y se han registrado como republicanos o votantes independientes, solamente 83 votaron en los comicios del 8 de mayo.

El partido republicano permite que personas registradas como republicanos o sin afiliación partidaria voten en sus comicios primarios.

En Henderson, esos primarios son equivalente a las elecciones generales de noviembre porque hay tan pocos demócratas en el condado que en la mayoría de los casos, los demócratas no nominan un candidato alternativo al republicano.

Hay un total de 1,991 personas votantes en el Condado Henderson que se han identificado como hispanos o latinos.

Tal vez hay más votantes hispanos que esta cifra porque identificar a su etnicidad es respuesta opcional en los trámites de registración de votantes en Carolina del Norte.

El tema del programa que se conoce como 287g se convirtió en punto polémico en los últimos días de la campaña entre McDonald y Griffin.

McDonald ha continuado el programa, que adiestra a carceleros locales para investigar el estatus migratorio de detenidos en el centro de detención local.

Durante un foro de candidatos, Griffin indicó que no automáticamente continuará esta colaboración con las autoridades de inmigración del Gobierno federal sin evaluar el programa.

Varios miembros de la comunidad hispana asistió a este foro, que empezó con el moderador del foro rehusando a leer una pregunta a los candidatos escrita en español.

El foro tuvo lugar días después de un operativo en el Condado Henderson y la región montañosa en que las autoridades de inmigración del Gobierno federal detuvieron a más de dos docenas de inmigrantes, inclusive de 14 del Condado Henderson.

La comunidad de activistas de Henderson respondieron a los arrestos por manifestarse frente a una oficina local del Servicio de Inmigración y Aduanas, o ICE, que se sitúa cerca del Hospital Pardee.

Felicia Arriaga, graduada de las escuelas públicas del Condado Henderson que ha estudiado el tema de 287g en Carolina del Norte, dijo que "no es sorprendente" la ausencia de hispanos en las casillas de Henderson el 8 de mayo.

Este otoño, Arriaga será maestra de sociología de Appalachian State University en Boone.

LA BAJA PARTICIPACIÓN de votantes hispanos en los comicios del 8 de mayo en Henderson gestiona que el tema de redadas carcelarias en el centro de detención de Henderson es más asunto de contraste para los activistas que los votantes.

Arriaga, graduada de la Universidad Duke en Durham, ha sido miembro de la comité de relaciones humanas de la ciudad de Durham.

"Creo que no hicieron esfuerzos para aumentar la votación de hispanos en el Condado Henderson," dijo Arriaga.

La semana pasada Griffin dijo que probablemente no continuará el programa 287g si no tiene la flexibilidad para enforcar solamente a los reos acusados de delitos graves o delitos menores violentos.

Bryan Cox, vocero del ICE, dijo que el acuerdo entre su agencia y ICE no otorga a Griffin tal discreción.

"Creo que todos los votantes registrados deben de participar en los comicios," dijo Griffin el lunes. "Las decisiones que tomaré no serán influenciadas por cómo la gente votó."

En entrevista con La Voz Independiente la semana pasada Griffin dijo que tomará una decisión sobre el futuro del 287g sin importar las consecuencias políticas.

Griffin se convertirá en alguacil el 3 de diciembre.

Merry Parris Guy, la presidenta del partido republicano del Condado Henderson, tampoco respondió a una llamada telefónica buscando su reacción a esa análisis.

Figure 3.2. "Muy pocos hispanos votaron." Courtesy of *La Voz Independiente*.

Kalir and Wissink (2016), these case managers justify their actions through a "concomitant move on the side of state-agents towards progressive political positions (adopting human rights discourse), compassionate attitudes (showing empathy for the 'victims' of the system), and a critical view of the state-system that is nonetheless accompanied by an overall acceptance that 'we work in a democratic country where the rules should be respected" (37).

Whether it's a cozy consensus or a collective amnesia (described more in chapter 4), particularly for more progressive local elected officials, over the span of about ten years, many actors failed to interrogate why their attitudes or even their "progressive political positions" did not lead to progressive policy changes. This sealed-off political realm contributes to a racial triangulation process, which places limitations on nonprofits and grassroots activists alike who may have similar imaginaries of citizenship but who ultimately still function within the immigrant rights silo, potentially limiting additional criminal justice reforms.

Of the three counties described in this chapter, Henderson and Cabarrus Counties elected a new sheriff in 2018, yet only in Henderson County did the immigration enforcement partnership become part of the narrative, although this did not necessarily translate to more traditional political participation as measured by voter turnout (Redaccion La Voz 2018). While we might expect that voter turnout would increase based on this issue, there are many factors to consider since voter turnout does not happen in a vacuum. Instead, intentional efforts from within and outside the Latinx electorate needed to be involved in voter education efforts to ultimately drive more Latinxs to participate in the political realm (fig. 3.2).

Of the 1,303 self-identified Hispanics registered to vote as Republicans or Independents in the county, only 83 voted. In Henderson County, only those registered as Republicans or Independents were able to vote in the May primary since no Democratic challenger ran. That is a small percentage of eligible voters who showed up to weigh in on an issue that largely impacts them.

What ultimately seals off this political realm is the inability for local electoral groups to consider how nonvoters factor into the framing of electoral campaigns. The exclusion from traditional measures of political participation (i.e., voting) provides a political opportunity for nonvoters and grassroots groups to participate in the political realm, whereas they are typically pushed out. In addition, many then choose to adopt contentious tactics—challenging candidates and seeking to disrupt campaign events (Tarrow 2011)— whereas mainstream groups do not often participate in the electoral process in similar ways. Even under a Democrat-led federal administration that implements immigration enforcement practices covertly, contentious groups, as Kalir and Wissick (2016) find in their work, are penalized because "actors who do articulate real alternatives [to the deportation continuum] are banned from the dominant political framework and dismissed as radical or utopian" (46).

## County Commissioner Knowledge

### HENDERSON COUNTY

Most discussions about the program in Henderson County took place during the initial implementation years of 2006–8. Beyond the 287(g) program, then sheriff Rick Davis would inform the county commissioners about the sheriff office's involvement in a worksite enforcement action in the fall of 2008 (Henderson County BOC 2008c). In 2009 and 2010, Sheriff Rick Davis would provide updates about the program to the commissioners, including statistics, charges of those arrested and detained, and the costs of the program. In 2009, the number of ICE detainees would also continue to be part of the discussion to expand the detention center (Henderson County BOC 2009). Surprisingly around this same time, issues of immigration discussed with the county commissioners included the U-Visa program and presentations by local faith leaders in 2010.[2] While local immigration enforcement often negatively impacts the lives of immigrants, U-Visas—nonimmigrant visas available to immigrant victims of certain crimes—are more of an immigrant integration tool that also promotes immigrant community involvement with local authorities like police.

During the 2009 discussions, representatives from the Immigrant Rights Coalition—Reverend Austin Rios and Zacnite Figueroa—presented to the commission and concluded with the following recommendations: uphold law enforcement accountability by focusing on (convicted) criminal aliens who pose a threat to public safety as stated in the memorandum of agreement (MOA); adopt a policy of citation for traffic violations and other minor misdemeanors; provide transparency by releasing current arrest and racial data and the costs of the 287(g) program to the public; and begin rebuilding trust with the Latinx community through collaborative crime prevention programs as alternatives to 287(g). The recommendations presented pushed for greater transparency and efforts to deter arrests for minor traffic violations. These perspectives also point out the racialized nature of the program, and to some extent, the members of the Immigrant Rights Coalition are also hopeful that there can be positive relationships with local law enforcement. Unfortunately, when immigrant rights groups advocate for the deportations of some immigrants, officials can seize that opportunity to justify the use of local immigration enforcement whenever they see fit. In other words, opening the door for a bad immigrant/good immigrant dichotomy, can be used to further target any immigrant.

In 2011, Sheriff Rick Davis began a leave for medical retirement, eventually resigning after a settlement with a female deputy who brought complaints against him (Moss 2013). The county commissioners appointed Charles McDonald "after the county Republican Party's executive committee recommended him from a field of 12 candidates" (Moss 2013). During his first year as sheriff, he presented information about the federal ICE building located in the county, but not under his supervision, and requested additional funding to expand the 287(g) program by adding a deputy. Oddly enough, the commission set two seemingly contradictory legislative goals later that year:

to support a North Carolina driver's permit for agricultural workers and to support suspension of mandatory use of E-Verify for agriculture.[3] In 2013, the sheriff's office stated that federal funding reimbursements for the program continued to decrease, down 30–40 percent from the previous fiscal year (July 17, 2013). This continued to be discussed in subsequent county commissioner meetings in early 2014, and by mid-2014, Steve Wyatt, the county manager at the time, noted in a meeting that the program could run on the previously generated revenue only for an additional year. He also reminded the board Henderson County Board of Commissioners meeting that "ICE was started as an Enterprise Fund" (Henderson County BOC 2014)—meant to generate revenue by housing immigrants for the federal government. The decline in support from the federal government also resulted in a decline in dedicated positions, meaning that employees were transitioning to other areas in the sheriff's office.

In April 2017, I attended two meetings where community members brought concerns about the program. One was the Latino Information Network (LINK) meeting on April 12, where law enforcement representatives were present to answer questions. In a volunteer role, I offered to take the notes and record it in order to accurately represent people's comments. In attendance were the Hendersonville chief of police, Chief Blake; Sheriff McDonald; the public information officer for the sheriff's office, Frank Stout; and the Laurel Park Police chief, Bobbi Trotter. The meeting concluded with questions about the possibility of using alternative forms of identification when interacting with local law enforcement when driver's licenses were invalid. Chief Trotter responded that she was interested in learning more, while Chief Blake's stance reflected that of the sheriff's office, as he raised concerns about the legitimacy of certain alternative forms of identification like the matricula consular—an identity card issued by a consulate to citizens residing outside of that country. These would all lead to a lot of interest in the 287(g) steering committee meeting set to take place on April 20, 2017.

The other meeting, on April 19, was a presentation by Pisgah Legal Services, an agency that provides free legal advice to underserved populations in Western North Carolina counties (Madison, Buncombe, Henderson, Transylvania, Rutherford, and Polk). Representatives from the organization were joined by Bert Lemkes—co-owner of the Van Wingerden Greenhouse Company and advocate for immigration reform from a business perspective—who described the economic importance of immigrants. In that forum, community members asked questions about the 287(g) program, rights for immigrants, and general immigration system concerns. Not present were immigrants themselves who could speak to their own experiences. Immigration attorneys are far and few between in the area, but the ones present alluded to their ongoing conversations with the sheriff's office. This particular forum lacked the per-spectives of those directly impacted community members.

According to the Henderson County 287(g) Steering Committee meetings, eighty-one individuals were "encountered," while twenty-nine were removed in 2016. In 2017, fifty-eight individuals were "encountered," and five were re-moved. Although the previously mentioned Immigration and Customs Fund no longer existed in the county budget, the sheriff's office continued to re-quest federal support for holding immigrants through the State Criminal Alien Assistance Awards (SCAAP). For the aforementioned years, the Bureau of Justice Assistance (BJA) awarded $16,361 and $6,832 through this program (SCAAP database). Although the Transactional Records Access Clearinghouse (TRAC) immigration data—the tool to learn more about federal immigra-tion enforcement—displays different time intervals than the data presented during the 287(g) program, for 2016, ICE sent twenty-seven detainers to the sheriff's office and eighty-one in 2017. These numbers do not match up to the previously reported numbers from the 287(g) steering committee meetings, making it extremely difficult to know just how many individuals were held in the Henderson County Detention Facility on detainer requests.

A year later, the 2018 Henderson County 287(g) Steering Committee meet-ing was one of the more heated exchanges I have witnessed. For starters, instead of being held at the detention center—consistent with previous years—it was held in a smaller room in the county courthouse, meaning that only about forty people were able to fit into the room (DeGrave 2018). As a response to ICE arrests earlier in the year, community members were also encouraged to attend the meeting, prompting additional ICE presence, in a pattern that would continue into 2019. At this meeting, five ICE officials were introduced (Chez Thompson, Joseph Fuentes, Robert Williams, Bryan Cox, and Steve LaRocca) along with the main point of contact between the Hender-son County Sheriff's Office and ICE, Lieutenant McDonald from the sheriff's office. The only substantial difference in this presentation than at previous meetings was Steve LaRocca's describing the February 2017 implementation memo under the new presidential administration and the implications for reporting. After an eight-minute presentation, community members asked questions about the prominence of "Hispanics" in the success stories, con-cerns about ICE detention conditions, and concerns about large-scale ICE arrests across the state.

To the last point, Bryan Cox continued to claim that these types of part-nerships were necessary to prevent more frequent at-large ICE arrests, a nar-rative that would persist across the state during the contentious 2018 sheriff elections discussed later in this book. According to Cox, "In a 287(g) county, there is a need for fewer at large arrests because ICE is able to take custody of persons who've been encountered in a jail. If 287(g) were not to exist, ice is required to enforce federal immigration law, in a county where that is not able to take place, where ICE is not allowed to have access to these local law enforcement facilities, that will necessitate an increase in at-large arrests." He did not emphasize the discretion these officials have to solely arrest those who they are looking to arrest. Not included in his comments is more information about the ICE reliance on these local-level partnerships because they do not have sufficient staff to go after every immigrant in the country. He also neglected to describe all the other communication that goes into ICE notification processes as described in chapter 2. Furthermore, this narrative is meant to create fear and panic in the community.

As the question-and-answer session continued, community members booed ICE officials' comments, particularly that "sheriffs want to keep their community safer. . . . You really should be supporting programs like this"; and "eighty-one people, I don't think that's traumatic for the community." Another community member, Nicole Townsend (who ran for city council in the neighboring city of Asheville) picked up this issue of trauma, pointed at the two ICE officers who were clearly non-white, and asked them to "come home." In response, Cox asked that community members not demonize ICE officers, since they are *just enforcing the law.* About an hour into the meeting, an older white woman stood up to ask a question, which ended with her telling Bryan Cox that "you can quit your job, if you felt like it," which received applause from the audience. He reminded her that he's not a political appointee but a career official. The last comment before people started to stand up and exit the room came from a Latinx woman, who stood up to say, "When are you going to stop demonizing us?" Some of the community members continued to speak to each other inside the room, while others approached the ICE officials to ask questions.[4]

GASTON COUNTY

In 2018, Sheriff Cloninger was entering his thirty-second year as sheriff and had never faced a competitive race for his seat. Cloninger is a registered Democrat. One former Gaston County commissioner—Representative John Torbett, now in his fifth term as a North Carolina House representative—was the most adamant supporter of the 287(g) program; he pushed to expand any local ICE partnerships to additional agencies like the county police force and to discontinue "all federally funded non-mandated programs servicing illegal residents" (Gaston County BOC 2006b, 17).[5] Indicative of the strong support for 287(g) programs moving forward from 2006, only one commissioner voted against the resolution, Commissioner Pearl Floyd, who raised concerns about possible legal repercussions. Prior to the implementation of the 287(g) program, as early as 2006, Sheriff Cloninger asked for financial support to pursue consultants capable of assisting in obtaining SCAAP awards. In county commissioner documents, the first mention I identified included approximately $4,000, set aside by the board of commissioners to pay consultants to assist in obtaining $23,987 in SCAAP awards (Gaston County BOC 2006a). Additional reimbursements continue for equipment, SCAAP awards, overtime funds, and the like.

As with other counties, in the beginning of 2008, the Gaston County Board of Commissioners heard a plea for a proposed jail expansion and new construction. ICE approached the county manager to consider a separate facility in which to house ICE detainees, a request that continues to be proposed across various counties in North Carolina. A motion passed to "authorize staff to interview and select a detention facility consultant to evaluate current and future jail needs and provide recommendations for addressing those anticipated needs" (Gaston County BOC 2008). The proposed consultant—a retired chief deputy and certified jail administrator from Mecklenburg County—was identified for his "familiarity with the ICE program, different levels of confinement, building configurations, experience and knowledge."

Common across the counties in this book, minimal information about the "success" of the program came to the board of commissioners. In February 2008, the sheriff made a brief presentation about the program, in which he noted that since June 2007, 302 individuals had been turned over to ICE, and the average interview time of individuals was about 4.15 hours. In summary, forty-five to fifty individuals were deported monthly, and the estimated housing fees were $30,000–$35,000. Complementing this 2008 update was an additional request to add a sergeant and two deputy positions. In board of commissioner meetings, the drain on local resources like the health department, hospital emergency room, and other county resources were often uplifted as immediate positives from these deportations, with no considerations of the negative impacts on the immigrant community. In 2010, Commissioner Torbett continued his anti-immigrant push by requesting support from other commissioners for Senate Joint Resolution 1349, "An Act to Create the Crime of Willful Failure to Carry or Complete an Alien Registration Document."

Over the years, the sheriff's office received SCAAP reimbursement funding for a variety of local expenses, including disaster preparedness, jail construction projects, training for detention officers, and education and training for incarcerated individuals. In a 2013 board of commissioners meeting (Gaston County BOC 2013), budget concerns led to a community survey on the proposed county budget.[6] One survey question asked whether individuals were in favor of eliminating the ICE program, which identifies and transports illegal immigrants to U.S. ICE enforcement facilities in Atlanta, and "saves"

$123,712; 21.6 percent of respondents were in favor. Of course, this question did not take into account who "saved" this money but implies that the program keeps tax dollars from being spent on immigrants. And 54.96 percent of respondents chose "Do not cut programs and accept recommended tax increase of 5.4 cents."

In that same budgetary season, the county manager recommended revisiting the funding for the 287(g) program along with a general reduction for the sheriff's office (2013–14 budget). Furthermore, the county manager made recommendations about the reliance on intergovernmental revenues, noting that "an overdependence on such revenues can be detrimental if federal and state funds cease. If intergovernmental revenues are eliminated or reduced, then the government has to decide between eliminating services or funding them with other revenues, such as the property tax" (Gaston County BOC 2013–14,102). In 2012, the sheriff's office earned over $1.2 million from housing federal prisoners in the county jail. In fiscal year 2013, this slightly decreased to $1.1 million. Although not the focus of this book, other financial considerations continue with the U.S. Marshal Service to house federal prisoners.

Edgar Vasquez—the 287(g) program manager—led the 2016 steering committee meeting on November 1, 2016, which lasted only about fifteen minutes. According to his information, since 2007, 23 officers had been trained, seven of whom were active officers at the time of that steering committee meeting, and 2 had participated in refresher training. In 2016, ICE identified 180 people and removed 47. Being, once again, the only non-ICE- or sheriff-affiliated person in the room for this steering committee meeting, I was able to ask a few additional questions after Edgar Vasquez's short presentation including concerning the breakdown of arrests by agencies (sheriff and police), more information about the "success" stories, county involvement in the implementation phases, and clarification about definitions used. Besides the updated numbers from 2016, he did not provide any new information. Most sheriff personnel present were not employed by the office when the 287(g) program began.

In 2016, the Priority Enforcement Program (PEP) categories were still being presented, meaning that the encounters indicated in table 1.1 could be broken down even further into priorities 1, 2, or 3 with corresponding descriptions (see previous chapter for more information about these and the changing classifications). Although this does not total the 180 indicated during the presentation, and later confirmed with a reporter who requested the information as well, 58 of these individuals were in the priority 1 category (threats to national security, border security, and public safety), 54 in the priority 2 category (those charged with misdemeanors and new immigration violators), and 74 in the priority 3 category (other immigrant violators). In a follow-up story in the *Gaston Gazette*, ICE spokesperson Bryan Cox commented that 16 of those people had been removed from the country, indicating that some of these individuals were possibly still in immigrant detention outside of the Gaston County Sheriff's Office at the time (Lawson 2017).

## CABARRUS COUNTY

Prior to the implementation of the 287(g) program in Cabarrus County in 2008, the board of commissioners voted to declare English as the official language of the county. The sheriff would also secure additional personnel to combat the gangs in the county. At the time, the sheriff's office was participating with the Charlotte/Mecklenburg Gang Task Force but did not have any dedicated personnel of their own. In this presentation to the board of commissioners, the sheriff conflated gang membership, being Hispanic, and illegality as rationales to justify an increase in personnel. In the 2007 board of commissioners budget report it was noted that "illegal Hispanics are increasing in population in Cabarrus County and with them come countless Cocaine traffickers, Methamphetamine, Heroin and Marijuana. This poses an imminent threat of continual growth of violent crime in this county" (152). The report also referred to a 2006 case in which a Cabarrus County sheriff's office patrol vehicle was shot at three times by an undocumented immigrant ("illegal alien," in their words) gang-identified affiliate, which provided additional rationale. For the sheriff's office, this also pushed them to consider personnel recruitment strategies: "Cabarrus County desperately needs to continue attracting minority applicants, especially foreign language speaking individuals" (Cabarrus County BOC 2007, 146). Although the hiring of Latinx personnel capable of speaking Spanish may assist the agency, it often is used to conceal racism and racially disproportionate outcomes of policing.

Furthermore, the explicit racism espoused in the beginning of the program also was driven by economic motivations. In the 2010 budget report, 400 foreign-born individuals resided in the jail. Of those, 350 were deported, and reimbursement for each of these individuals was set at $63.00 per day (Cabarrus County BOC 2010). Noted in the FY2010 category "Major Accomplishments and challenges," the sheriff's office received over $20,000 in SCAAP reimbursements from the BJA for holding immigrants in the local jail. In fiscal years 2012 and 2013, the sheriff's department requested initial funding for an ICE transportation program. Prior to this request, sheriff personnel were transporting immigrants outside of their normal duties, increasing overtime and officer fatigue, but "the reimbursement should cover most all transport costs, and will benefit the Sheriff's Office by eliminating the need for off-duty on-call schedule, reducing overtime expenses, and leaving on-call Patrol in the community for increased availability and public protection"

(Cabarrus County BOC 2014). In 2014, the sheriff's office was able to bring in $4,446.75 in revenue through the 287(g) program. However, in 2015, it was cut in half, and in the fiscal year 2017 budget proposal, significant revenues from the program were not expected. Toward the end of 2017, the lack of revenue was described as "this decrease is the result of ICE initiatives, which reduces the offenses that are fully processed (Cabarrus County BOC 2018). But for the 2018 fiscal year budget, more optimism was expressed: "These initiatives have already begun changing with the change in this Country's leadership and it is expected to increase this amount for Fiscal Year 2018" (265). While reimbursements for holding immigrants in the jail decreased over time, sheriff personnel were optimistic that the Trump administration would increase these reimbursements and thereby make incarcerating immigrants profitable once again. Aside for the occasional budgetary update for the county commission, little information was provided about the program until the steering committee meetings began in 2015.

The February 23, 2016, the Cabarrus County 287(g) Steering Committee meeting occurred a short time after a forum in Charlotte, North Carolina, discussing immigration enforcement and the 2016 ICE arrests of recently arrived, mostly Central American youth. In one of these instances, in January of 2016, Wildin Acosta was picked up while he was waiting for his school bus.[7] While the projector was being set up at the meeting, Bryan Cox and other ICE officials were discussing that forum and follow-up items that they needed to pass along to news stations WRAL and Univision. At one point, one of these officials said, "I thought they were going to come," which I assume referred to protests and angry community members from the recent forum. In subsequent steering committee meetings, ICE officials would take some time before the official start of the meetings to attempt to explain Wildin and the other young people's situations: they had all recently aged out of the category of protected recent arrival youth and were thereby legally vulnerable.

In this February 2016 meeting, Edgar Vasquez gave the overview of the program, the priorities under PEP, and basic statistics of the program. Then I asked questions about the relationships between the sheriff's office and the Latinx community. One sergeant mentioned that the office was open to working with community members but did not offer concrete plans to do so.

## 287(G) REMOVAL OVERVIEW

As time went on, the summary data presented at steering committee meetings became less detailed, and in some instances data was not available for meetings that took place earlier in the year. Table 3.1 provides summary information about encounters and removals in 2016 and 2017 for Henderson, Gaston, and Cabarrus Counties. In all three locations, the percent of

Table 3.1. 287(g) encounters and removal proceedings in Cabarrus, Gaston, and Henderson Counties, fiscal years 2016 and 2017

| | 2016 Encounters | 2016 Removals | 2016 Percentage of removals | 2017 Encounters | 2017 Removals | 2017 Percentage of removals |
|---|---|---|---|---|---|---|
| **Cabarrus County** | | | | | | |
| | 142 | 46 | 32 | 173 | 18 | 10 |
| **Gaston County** | | | | | | |
| | 186 | 64 | 34 | 187 | 16 | 9 |
| **Henderson County** | | | | | | |
| | 81 | 29 | 36 | 82 | 51* | 37 |
| **State total** | | | | | | |
| | 3,551 | 777 | 22 | 3,714 | 269 | 7 |

*While 51 individuals were placed into removal proceedings, 30 were deported, according to the 2018 Steering Committee meeting.

immigrants removed from the county was higher than the state percentage, suggesting a more aggressive effort by ICE to pick up these individuals. The steering committee meetings in 2017 then led to some community interest in the 2018 sheriff elections.

## 2018 Elections

In Gaston County, Sheriff Cloninger, running as a Democrat, did not face a challenger in the 2018 election. In Cabarrus County, five Republican candidates originally ran for the sheriff's seat in the 2018 primary. Of those, only one candidate—Adam Peck—would highlight his focus on immigration in his biography submitted to the *Independent Tribune* (Staff Reports 2018a). Prior to this election, Sheriff Brad Riley—a Democrat—held the position for almost a decade and endorsed Van Shaw in his retirement letter. Van Shaw won the Republican primary with 65.31 percent of the vote and faced Gary Rodgers, the Democratic candidate, in the general election (Staff Reports 2018b). Van Shaw's responses to the *Independent Tribune* included an emphasis on community outreach programs, transparency, and his previous experience working for the North Carolina Bureau of Investigation as well as his current position as the chief deputy within the Cabarrus County Sheriff's Office (Huddle 2018). He did not publicly include any campaign issues focusing on immigration or immigration enforcement. In that same questionnaire, Gary Rodgers would not provide responses, but Van Shaw noted Rodgers's "inexperience" as a law enforcement officer. Experience is not a requirement to run for sheriff in North Carolina. Van Shaw won the general election with 60 percent of the vote to Rodgers's 40 percent (Staff Reports 2018c). While the Cabarrus and Gaston County 2018 Sheriff elections were not contentious, the Henderson County sheriff election was.

On April 17, 2018, I attended the Henderson County Sheriff Candidate Forum along with about thirty other Latinx community members. Held in the auditorium at the local community college—a place where I had previously given a keynote speech to a group of Latinx high school students for College Access Day—the packed event covered questions of immigration, body camera footage, school safety, and staffing concerns (Lacey 2018). As is the case when I return home, I often know the community members who engage in these conversations. In a truly participatory fashion, they had many questions for the candidates, probably more than the mostly white attendees in the room. Questions concerned their stance on the 287(g) program, what programs would be offered for immigrants, and commentary on the lack of cultural competency in the office. We all sat in a corner of the room, and I asked the ushers (I previously served as a moderator for similar forums in Chatham County) if only questions written in English would be accepted. They responded in the affirmative, and I proceeded to help translate this group's questions so that they too could participate in the process.

Unfortunately, we somehow missed one note card and left it in Spanish alone, and the moderator decided to home in on that oversight. In what you can imagine was not perfect Spanish, he read the question and then responded in English, "This forum will be in English, and any questions submitted in Spanish will not be read," to which there was thundering applause and my stomach sank. And that was only the beginning of the forum.

This forum took place in the wake of ICE raids and arrests in the area, which further pushed Latinx community members to attend. Eventually both candidates were able to discuss the 287(g) program and immigration more broadly. Sheriff Charles McDonald, an avid supporter of the Trump administration, maintained the program's usefulness for the county, while the incumbent, Lowell Griffin, differed on this issue; he linked the program to fears within the Latinx community, who, he noted, greatly contribute to the economy of the county. Griffin said, "There are actually industries here that would fold without these folks. We have to have a relationship. I would actually like to establish a liaison for the Latinx community. We have to

earn trust. . . . They can help us root out the bad actors in their community"
(Moss 2018).

Furthermore, this challenger, who would unseat the sitting sheriff with 59
percent of the vote, told the crowd that he would look into the program and
that he wasn't very familiar with it. This encouraged some community members that Griffin would be more open to conversations once he took office.
The sheriff made a few other comments about the necessity of the program
including, "It's not arbitrary: Everybody that comes in gets run through the
system" (Feldblum 2018). Disagreeing with these comments, many of the Latinx community members stood up and marched out of the forum to gather
outside and discuss the candidates' responses. Once outside, a staff member
with the Asheville-based group Compañeros Inmigrantes de las Montañas
en Accion (CIMA) and El Centro Henderson County spoke to the community
members about the 287(g) program and its local impacts, commenting on the
ten years of the program and the relationship to the ICE raids that had taken
place the week before.

A few months later in early June, community members in Henderson
County, led by an organizer from Southerners on New Ground, coordinated
with Mijente, a national digital-organizing hub, as part of its Chinga La Migra
Tour to be the first stop in North Carolina before the group headed to Alamance County. The stop in Alamance County would be the culmination
of the tour in order to protest McDonald, the most anti-immigrant sheriff
in North Carolina. The protest in Henderson County was directed at Sheriff
McDonald but was also a means to set out expectations for the sheriff-elect.
This kind of activism was necessary during and after the election, particularly because the sheriff candidates were not willing to get rid of the 287(g)
program.

Later in June, I was contacted by a local reporter who was concerned that
the Latinx community did not come out to vote, even though he felt that the
issue of immigration was clearly something that should have brought them
out. After some consideration, I respectfully replied that very few groups conducted Get Out the Vote (GOTV) efforts in the Latinx and Spanish-speaking
communities even when there was lots of attention on them (Redaccion La
Voz 2018). Moreover, when there are constant racialized burdens to contend
with in the traditional political realm, these voters may rationalize their participation in democracy in other ways. While the ability to shift the sheriff's
stance on the 287(g) program was out of reach, community members turned
their attention to the county commissioners.

The groups in Henderson County saw the clear connections between the
sheriff, ICE officials, and county commissioners. I would continue to witness
this at the beginning of 2019 when discussions heated up during the 2019

county budget proposal presentations and sessions. Throughout 2019, the American Civil Liberties Union (ACLU) of North Carolina, the Immigration Network of Henderson County, and the League of Women Voters continued to provide opportunities for community participation. In the fall of 2019, they put on a three-part "civil discourse" series, "Immigration 101: Facts vs. Fiction": "The Myth of Duplicated Services"; "Storytelling: The Myth of 'Just Get in Line'"; and "Undocumented Immigrant Population: Economic/Crime Myths." They also held a press conference about the program on June 4, 2019, and coordinated turnout for the 287(g) steering committee meeting held on December 10, 2019.

## Reinforcing Persistence through Community Participation

Early in 2019, the newly elected Henderson County sheriff, Lowell Griffin, ignited controversy by suggesting that the 287(g) program was no longer fiscally responsible and then hiring a Latinx community advocate. By hiring this advocate, he could begin to outreach to the Latinx community and distance himself from accusations of an office that racializes immigrants. Although he lacked expertise when it came to the 287(g) program, shortly after taking office, he brough the issue of sustainability to the Henderson County Board of Commission. Instead of supporting his decision to end the program because of financial constraints, the board encouraged him to keep the program by insisting that they could find an additional $250,000 to keep the program going. In May, I attended one of these budget hearings and make a public comment regarding the history of the program in the county, highlighting the impact on families, the budgetary impacts for the community, and the lack of accountability for the sheriff's office. I stayed long enough at that meeting to hear one community member express his anger with the county commissioners for continuing the program.

In March 2019, about three months after Sheriff Griffin took office, a local reporter compared him with the neighboring sheriff Quentin Miller, in Buncombe County. I met Sheriff Miller in February, 2019, while attending a community meeting in Asheville, North Carolina, and learned that he would be ending detainers within the coming weeks. Most sheriffs in North Carolina and across the country honor ICE detainers, but most do not have a 287(g) program. Although that sheriff ran a campaign on a no-287(g) platform, it was a bit confusing since the office did not have one at the time and, to my knowledge, the previous sheriff was not keen on the program. Instead, this maneuver was meant to both distance him from the policy in neighboring Henderson County and to highlight a good-faith effort to work with the local immigrant community. Furthermore, his policy changes would include a move to end to detainers, consideration of his role in other Department of Homeland Security (DHS) investigations, and eventually hiring a Latinx immigrant for his public affairs team.[8] He eventually joined many of his newly elected counterparts across the state in standing by their decisions and pushing back against statewide legislation in House Bill 270, Sheriffs to Cooperate with ICE, a proposal that did not pass that year.

In 2019, the ACLU of North Carolina collaborated with local organizations in Henderson County to increase awareness of the program. As previously mentioned, in response to mounting pressure, the sheriff's office hired a Latinx liaison to assist in issues related to the Latinx community, encouraging the community to not fear officers and to report crimes. The ACLU of North Carolina continues to monitor this program along with the other three existing 287(g) programs, but in Gaston and Cabarrus Counties, community pressure hasn't developed in the same manner as in Henderson County.

# CHAPTER 4

# Collective Amnesia

## WHITE INNOCENCE AND IGNORANCE IN THE DEVOLUTION OF IMMIGRATION ENFORCEMENT

"That was during a different administration," said former Henderson County sheriff Charles McDonald during an April 12, 2017, Latino Information Network meeting in Hendersonville, North Carolina. While the statement just as easily applies to the state- or federal-level stance on local immigration enforcement practices, he repeated it a few times in this meeting. His aim? To reassure community members that the explicit targeting of Latinx immigrants in the county that had occurred back in 2008—characteristic of localities adopting local immigration enforcement partnerships around this time—was no longer occurring. Yet these shared memories of the program had divergent impacts on community members.

Moreover, these policy changes initiated almost fifteen years ago (2006–8) have become normalized and gone unchallenged as part of legal and state violence (Menjívar and Abrego 2012a) directed at Latinxs and Latinx immigrants alike in locales where 287(g) programs were adopted across the country. This chapter shows that, while the 287(g) program was visible in the beginning, it became invisible through normalized enforcement practices and the subsequent *collective amnesia* of the program's impetus. Furthermore, community members faced competing priorities, which prevented community members from maintaining a sustained resistance against such implementation.

Charles Mills (2007, 29) suggests that collective amnesia, as it pertains to race, allows for "conflicting judgements about what is important in the past and what is unimportant." According to Mills,

> if we are to understand collective memory, we also need to understand collective amnesia. Indeed, they go together insofar as memory is necessary selective—out of the infinite sequence of events, some trivial, some momentous, we extract what we see as the crucial ones and organize them into an overall narrative. . . . Thus there will be both official and

counter-memory, which conflicting judgements about what is important in the past and what is unimportant, what happened and does matter, what happened and does not matter, and what did not happen at all. So applying this to race, there will obviously be an intimate relationship between white identity, white memory, and white amnesia, especially about non-white victims. (29)

The previous chapters analyzed some of the official narrative documented in county documents and expressed by local and federal officials. For example, the "success" stories in the steering committees allows for federal and local actors to create a justifiable memory of the program without grappling with the cases where impacted community members disagree with the removal outcome. In addition, nowhere in the county documents is there material that memorializes the negative impacts of the 287(g) program. Instead, community members are forced to create their own narratives in hopes of creating a countermemory.

Although the relationship between white identity, white memory, and white amnesia are easily identified in other arenas of our country's collective memory of race issues, taken together, these frames can help explain the maintenance of local immigration enforcement practices. In addition to Mills's three frames of white identity, white memory, and white amnesia, I suggest a fourth frame: white ignorance. In doing so, I draw from Mills's development of the term "white ignorance," which he describes as "ignorance to cover both false belief and the absence of true belief," including the spread of misinformation within the group identity and social practices of whites (Mills 2007, 16). In *The Racial Contract*, Mills also describes this phenomena as "a cognitive model that precludes self-transparency and genuine understanding of social realities" (Mills 1997, 10). He notes that this ignorance stems from the centrality of race in the non-knowing and that this racialized causality covers interpersonal and social-structural instances. Furthermore, he states, "white ignorance need not always be based on bad faith. Obviously from the point of view of a social epistemology, especially after the transition from de jure to de facto white supremacy, it is precisely this kind of white ignorance that is most important" (Mills 2007, 21).

Other scholars note specific conditions like personal interests and structural constraints that help to cultivate and preserve ignorance (McGoey 2012; Mueller 2017). Both of these conditions require some form of negotiation at the personal, interpersonal, and organizational levels, particularly when whites are confronted with information that challenges their social realities. Although much of the literature on white ignorance pertains to whites

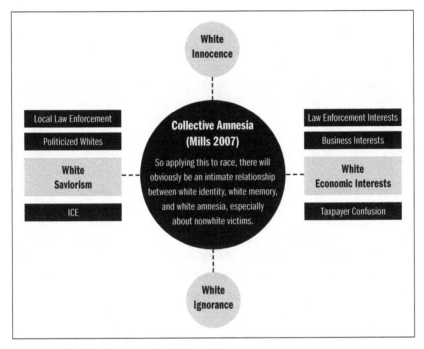

Figure 4.1. "Collective amnesia" chart.

negotiating their own beliefs about race, less has been written about the collective amnesia and selective memory of racist justifications for immigration enforcement as they occur "on the ground" (Delgado and Stefancic 2000).

Although many legal scholars focus on the racialized history of immigration policy construction at the federal level, little research in sociology exists that ties those federal-level histories to localized racist histories of adoption and implementation. This chapter, then, both identifies the collective amnesia of racist justifications for local immigration enforcement and tracks the frames used in this process throughout North Carolina, a state known as the testing ground and early adopter of many immigrant enforcement partnerships. The devolution of federal immigration enforcement throughout the United States places the ability to implement new practices into the hands of local law enforcement and local governments. In this process, local governments initially approved the implementation of partnerships with federal authorities for blatantly racist rationales of local law enforcement agencies. But few were willing to look back into that collective memory to grapple with those justifications. And the few that did have little to say about the normalization of the operations (fig. 4.1).

## Racist Beginnings

As discussed in the previous chapter, of the five counties studied, in three (Mecklenburg, Henderson, and Gaston) the sheriff's request to enter into 287(g) agreements was initiated by a formally appointed committee or by a resolution meant to assess the impact of "illegals" or racialized immigrants within the county. In Gaston County, recommendations were introduced by Commissioner Torbett under the resolution "To Adopt Policies and Apply Staff Direction Related to Illegal Residents in Gaston County" on November 9, 2006, during a county commissioner meeting, adopting the rationale that the commissioners "must look out for the health and welfare of the legal citizens of Gaston County."

In Henderson County, members of the Blue Ribbon Committee on Illegal Immigration mutually agreed to support the sheriff's proposal to adopt the 287(g) program in order to "collect and evaluate immigration data from county departments, particularly Health, Social Services, Schools, and Law Enforcement, especially as new immigration laws are enacted and/or old laws are enforced." This committee also suggested somewhat contradictory recommendations, such as a follow-up citizens committee, employee verification programs, formulation of statements about not welcoming illegal immigration, pushing Congress to reform immigration laws, and "recogniz[ing] the economic contributions of our Hispanic labor force to our county's economy." Not surprisingly, a few members of the Blue Ribbon Committee also proposed a minority report of recommendations, including the immediate implementation of the 287(g) program; the immediate implementation of the federal Employment Eligibility Verification Program (now E-Verify); implementation of the Systematic Alien Verification for Entitlements (SAVE) system in hospitals; "establish[ing] a long-range planning committee consisting of qualified County employees to determine the impact of immigration on Henderson County schools, infrastructure, budgets, and taxes"; phasing out employment of "illegal" immigrants within three to five years; and that future committees consist only of "U.S. citizens registered to vote in Henderson County" (Henderson County BOC 2007a).

In 2007, in Mecklenburg County, the Charlotte mayor's Immigration Study Commission was charged to "analyze the impact of immigration on Charlotte's (and [the] region's) quality of life, public safety, and economic opportunities" (Mayor's Immigration Study Commission 2007). The commission established four areas of study: public safety, economic development / workforce, education, and health care. They mainly highlighted the fiscal costs in these arenas. Although this commission conflated the costs of Hispanics and "illegal" immigrants, they ultimately proposed twenty-six recommendations, many of which reiterate the negative impact of immigrants and the need for enforcement to protect citizens both physically and financially. In total, this study commission produced nine public safety recommendations, three economic development / workforce recommendations, three education recommendations, four health-care recommendations, and three general recommendations. One member of this task force (a former Charlotte City Council member) concluded that although they ultimately supported the implementation of the 287(g) program, they wanted "light enforcement." This initial desire for "light enforcement" stands in stark contrast to the deportation efforts underway from 2006 to 2018, where the Mecklenburg County Sheriff's Office deported the highest number of immigrants in the state.

Although more attention—from media and community members— surrounded the initiation of the 287(g) programs from 2006 to 2008, other opportunities existed in which to revive concerns about the devolution of decision-making power of local governments regarding immigration-related practices and to reassess the blatantly racist impetus of the programs. One community member involved in the Blue Ribbon Committee on Illegal Immigration, in Henderson County, described how sheriff's officers would sit outside of the local clinic frequented by Mexican immigrants in the first few years of the 287(g) program, which inspired community members to attend county commission meetings to voice their grievances (Henderson County BOC 2007a). In Gaston County, three community members also opposed the initial implementation and sent a request to the county commissioners to rescind the aforementioned resolution (Gaston County BOC 2006c).

Commissioner Floyd of Gaston County and Commissioner Mark Williams of Henderson County raised questions about the rights of immigrants and potential legal battles. Yet these concerns were quieted by other commissioners, using arguments similar to Chairman Moyer's statement that there were a "lot of safeguards in the MOA [memorandum of agreement] with respect to the protection of the rights of the people involved, citizens of the community and appeal processes. This will not be a break into places and arrest people without due procedures. If we are not satisfied with how it's going we can terminate immediately. The downside is that the Federal Government can also terminate at anytime without paying us" (Henderson County BOC 2008b). The commissioners' justifications to each other overcame the limited concerns for the rights of immigrants. In addition, the possibility of legal battles were also dismissed. And these concerns would not resurface, at least not at the board of commissioners.

Although the county and city task forces and study commissions were asked to make recommendations during the initial implementation phase of the 287(g) program, they were not tasked with the responsibility to follow up with such recommendations, which further contributed to a collective amnesia regarding the implementation of the program. When county commissioners failed to create follow-up and oversight mechanisms, the only accountability and public engagement came from the entities implementing the recommendations, meaning that for immigration enforcement purposes, the responsibility lies with the various sheriff's departments themselves. Beginning in 2015, Immigration and Customs Enforcement (ICE) included a mandate for local law enforcement to hold annual steering committee meetings within the MOAs.

## Becoming Invisible

In retroactive interviews and community forums, whites minimized the initial implementation of these 287(g) programs and the blatant racist and xenophobic language predominantly voiced by their sheriffs, and sometimes by their counterparts on the county board. Local law enforcement in particular distanced themselves from those initial rationales and attempted to maintain their "law and order" approach. This is consistent with Amada Armenta's findings in Tennessee, where she describes local law enforcement as "by-the-books administrator[s]" and the "public protector[s]" (2012, 11–16). She finds that by-the-books administrators believe they have limited authority when implementing immigration laws and are fairly implementing the law by not employing discretion. Simultaneously, the public protector feels confident that the removal of "criminals" from the community serves to protect the larger community. Because the crimmigration entities did not experience a moral dissonance at the personal level, they could go on about their daily lives without questioning the rationales and implementation. As Mills notes, "whites will then act in racist ways while thinking of themselves as acting morally. In other words, they will experience genuine cognitive difficulties in recognizing certain behavior patterns as racist so that quite apart from the question of motivation and bad faith, they will be morally handicapped simply from the conceptual point of view in seeing and doing the right thing" (2007, 21).

Over the next ten years after initial program implementation, the funding component would also become less visible and not be discussed as deeply as in the initial years, marking an absence in the collective memory. Occasionally county sheriffs in these five counties would request county commissioners to appropriate funds for costs related to ICE expenses. These costs are further detailed in chapter 3 and 5, although it is unclear whether these costs were directly related to the 287(g) partnership, since other partnerships, data sharing, and communication with ICE were also occurring. Over the course of this period, various financial exchanges occurred between ICE, the county boards of commissioners, and the local law enforcement offices, both the sheriff and the police. Political scientists describe how community members make choices to not monitor the implementation of certain policies through rational ignorance (Robbins, Simonsen, and Feldman 2008). Instead, they rely on local elected officials (both county commissioners and sheriffs) to maintain authority over the decision-making process of the implementation of programs like immigration enforcement. Because the county commissioners approved the initial hiring of new sheriff deputies who would become deputized with ICE authority, this budgetary component of the 287(g) program was available for the public to access as shown in chapter 3. These budget line items sometimes included additional costs for updated technology, additional transportation costs, and additional personnel costs.

Aside from direct costs allocated to individual local governments and local law enforcement agencies, strategic planning efforts to construct jails were also brought to the county boards of commissioners with explicit input from ICE and U.S. marshals about rental space. For example, in an August 14, 2007, Mecklenburg County Commissioners meeting, building a new facility was brought up for discussion. Explicit in this discussion was a commitment from ICE to rent space within the newly constructed jail facility. So not only was the initial adoption of these programs based on racial justifications, but also the continuation of the program would explicitly rely on the incarceration of racialized immigrants over time.

Over the span of ten years, immigration enforcement reimbursement decisions were made during county commissioner meetings, particularly in Gaston and Henderson Counties. This means that financial aspects of the 287(g) program and other collaborations with ICE were publicly available for invested community members to identify and question. Yet the community members I interviewed, who had previously participated in initial push-back efforts, were unaware of such matters. Another example is in the Henderson County budget passed each year from 2008 to 2015, which included an Immigration and Customs Fund. This fund ranged from a low of approximately $600,000 in fiscal year 2011 to a high of approximately $825,000 in the 2012–13 budget. In 2015, the fund was closed, and the remaining amount of approximately $475,000 was moved into the general fund. This decision coincided with the end of the transportation agreement between ICE and the Henderson County Sheriff's Office, the closure of which program the public information officer rationalized as its "no longer being good stewards of taxpayer funds."[1]

As previously mentioned, community members highlighted the blatant policing of locations where many Latinx immigrants frequented. Yet, once that overt form of policing subsided, it became harder for Latinx community members to identify the more covert practices that were occurring. At the peak of the 287(g) program implementation, similar overt practices occurred in Alamance County, leading to the coordinated community response that would eventually result in the Department of Justice ending the program in 2012.

Not surprisingly, many of the local elected officials involved in the implementation of the 287(g) program have made their way into decision-making positions at the state level, where they have maintained a sense of ignorance of the impacts of such programs. During their time spent at the North Carolina General Assembly, two of these individuals (then representative Chuck McGrady of Henderson County and Representative Torbett of Gaston County) have failed to voice concerns about the programs in their respective counties—failing to see and do the right thing, even when a proposed statewide bill would implement the program across the state. Perspectives from both the governor's office and congressional representatives are strikingly similar, although one congressional representative—David Price—agreed that the program took on a life of its own after it was introduced in his committee at the federal level. While some white people may express their reluctant role in the program, others preferred to normalize the program's existence if it did not interfere with their economic motivations.

## Keeping It Invisible for Economic Motivations

The normalization and invisibility of the program also protects white economic interests and benefits majority-white communities. In community input sessions, business representatives expressed concerns about the negative impact of extra immigration enforcement. Those in the businesses that relied on immigrant labor—undocumented and legal—were eager to continue growing their businesses without the possibility of losing workers to deportation.

However, their concerns about the negative impact of immigration enforcement were not raised regarding the additional income resulting from detaining and housing undocumented immigrants. Of course, that county-level income still benefitted whites, especially those who relied heavily on law enforcement. In the initial years of implementation, incentives to detain and house individuals also came from state and national entities.

Henderson County was the only 287(g) program heavily dependent on agricultural work like harvesting apples. Henderson County is responsible for 85 percent of North Carolina's apple crop, harvested by some of the approximately 150,000 farmworkers in the state (Herrington 2020). On average, North Carolina farmworkers only make $11,000 per year, meaning that the profits from the harvests often go to corporations. Harsher enforcement might shift that, not only for Henderson County, but the other counties in the state would also face negative consequences from anti-immigrant worker legislation. To the extent that this is expected, the North Carolina Farm Bureau steps in to lobby against those bills that would make it easier to deport this class of workers. In one 287(g) program county—Henderson County—local agricultural businesses would often step in to support immigration reform legislation at the federal level. In one instance, in 2017, they wrote a letter to their federal lawmakers stating, "Congress must pass legislation that preserves agriculture's experienced workforce by allowing current farm workers to earn legal status." The letter continues: "For future needs, legislation must create an agricultural worker visa program that provides access to a legal and reliable workforce moving forward. This visa program needs to be market-based and have the flexibility to meet the needs of producers, including those with year-round labor needs, such as dairy and livestock" (Lacey 2017). The needs of the producers are front and center, with little regard for the immigrants themselves.

Around the same time, to highlight this contradiction, U.S. senator Thom Tillis took a tour of to a dairy farm to meet with thirty area farmers. Tillis commented, "Their survival really depends on whether or not we get it right. There are millions of positions that can only be filled by guest workers because first off we are at a high rate of employment, but we simply do not have people at these farm operations lining up. If we don't start recognizing this industry and our ability to grow food . . . we (will) rely on other countries to provide. This is not a place the United States wants to be" (Moores 2017). Tillis notes the U.S. dependency on migrant farmwork, a dependency that also stabilizes the agricultural sector.

This economic argument—wanting immigrant labor—was one of the only areas cited as a "positive" aspect of increased immigration to these counties. In eastern North Carolina, state representatives—led by Senator Brent Jackson, who also owns a larger farm, pushed legislation in the 2017 Farm Bill meant to dissuade organizing and collective bargaining agreements of farmworkers—particularly those affiliated with the Farm Labor Organizing Committee (FLOC) (Bouloubasis 2017). FLOC president Baldemar Velasquez emphasized this self-serving purpose: "Politicians that are also growers shouldn't pass self-serving laws simply because they don't want their workers to unionize" (SPLC 2017). In effect, the law prohibits agricultural producers from signing agreements with a union relating to a lawsuit and bars farmworker unions from entering into agreements with employers to have union dues transferred from paychecks, which would force FLOC to collect individual member dues and would take significant resources.

In 2021, a federal court blocked the North Carolina Farm Act of 2017 after a lawsuit was filed by the Southern Poverty Law Center (SPLC) and other civil rights groups, claiming that the law violates First Amendment rights to participate in unions (SPLC 2017). In some ways, farmwork is "protected" from the same E-Verify processes—a web-based way to check an employee's eligibility to work in the United States—that targeted larger pork and poultry factories like Smithfield in eastern North Carolina back in 2007 (Collins 2007). Unfortunately, this lack of protection also keeps them in a precarious position as demonstrated in recent hurricanes. During Hurricane Florence in September 2018, for example, migrant workers called 911 for help, but instead of listening to these individuals directly, emergency services communicated with their employer, who told them the workers "had everything they needed as far as food and water" (Hernandez 2018a; see also Hernandez 2018b).Their cries for help went unmet, emblematic of the unjust treatment farmworkers face on a regular basis throughout the state. While some whites expressed their explicit motivations to uphold white supremacy and capitalism, others preferred to play the victim.

## White Innocence and Perceived Costs to Community

Jamie Longazel (2014) found throughout his research in Hazelton, Pennsylvania—another new immigrant destination—that the "white majority manages not only to avoid culpability for having contributed to the hostility engendered by the Latinx threat narrative but also to present itself as victimized by this perceived invasion" (584). County commissioners and committees in North Carolina described the cost to them when it came to hypothetical services that could be used by immigrants throughout various counties. In Gaston County, Commissioner Torbett justified the implementation of the 287(g) program in the following way: "[Gaston] County has a limited supply of incoming revenue from ad valorem taxes; services to County citizens become limited when illegals extract funds for services, would like to meet with listed departments to work toward implementation, if adopted; do not know impact or number of illegal aliens residing in-County; not allowed to ask if legal/illegal; must look out for the health and welfare of the legal citizens of Gaston County" (Gaston County BOC 2006b).

Similarly, the Blue Ribbon Commission in Henderson County focused on the economic impacts of losing the workforce, arguing this imposed "a hard to measure cost loading on health care, social services, law enforcement, and schools systems." They also included sometimes-contradictory information, such as "The county's unemployment rate is 3.3%, well below the national average. It does not appear that in our county at this time, there is any measurable negative impact on jobs for resident citizens, nor even on pay levels for similar work. However, there is reasonable concern that such negative impact could be happening here and in other parts of the USA" (Henderson County BOC 2007a). Immigrants are often scapegoats during economic crisis, but this is less so the case during stable economic times.

Community members were often the only ones considering a more ethical approach to enforcement practices. Community representatives in Henderson County considered their responsibility for their fellow community members—pushing for more integrative initiatives. Of the commissioners, Commissioner Ward of Wake County was the one anomaly during the initial adoption of the program. She wanted to maintain a sense of white innocence and asked the Wake County sheriff what would happen to any children involved in situations where their caregiver was taken into jail and subsequently entered into deportation proceedings:

> Commissioner Ward: If you discover that a man, any man, that is perhaps here and doesn't have the legal documentation and they have a family—a wife and children, do you do anything beyond take care of the person and place them in a position to go back to their country? Do you do anything with the wife and children? That always bothers me—because they're left so hopeless and helpless.

> Sheriff Donnie Harrison: That's entirely up to ICE, let me back up and tell you this. We treat everybody the same—I use the term feed them out of the same spoon. If we stop someone on the road or if we have a warrant for somebody and we pick them up and they have children or whatever—we treat them just like we would you if you had children in your car. We make sure that someone comes and picks those children up if the parent says it's okay for them to go with. What you're getting at—if they're going to be deported—that's up to ICE. They do—when a person leaves us and goes into ICE's custody, ICE notifies the people plus the person that has been picked up has the right to use the phone just like everything else—there's paperwork he or she has to fill out so sometimes you hear that the family don't know where they are, that's because evidently they don't talk to their family. Because we do and ICE does, and the paperwork that they fill out and the lawyers—they know where they are. (Wake County BOC 2008, 3:16–18)

Here, Commissioner Ward grapples with the ethics in separating families and her role in it, very much like Commissioner Floyd of Gaston County and Commissioner Williams of Henderson County grappled with the legal questions regarding the initial implementation of the program. But again, nothing in the official record leads me to believe they considered themselves acting immorally.

Some local law enforcement even claimed that their current practices are much better than those of their previous counterparts. In a 2017 community forum in Henderson County, representatives from the sheriff's office maintained that the initial adoption of the program was the result of a "bad apple" in the previous sheriff's administration. Yet they say little about the Henderson County Board of Commissioners' involvement in the program, excusing them from culpability. In various interviews and public settings, community members referred to the previous sheriff—Sheriff Rick Davis—as racist for his implementation of the program, while local law enforcement simply stated, "That was under a different administration" (April 12, 2017, LINK [Latino Information Network] meeting in Henderson County, recording).

During a meeting where the sheriff's office and local police departments in Henderson County were asked to provide information at the LINK meeting—a monthly meeting of advocates working in the Latinx community, community members (both older white individuals and Latinx individuals—mostly direct service providers) asked a variety of questions of law enforcement officials. The public information officer for the sheriff's office emphasized their willingness to work with the Latinx community, something that was also conveyed by other local law enforcement agencies across the state, yet little evidence pointed to goodwill between the Latinx community and the sheriff's office. After an opportunity to answer questions from the audience, that same public information officer, Frank Stout, later on seem to feel attacked and commented, "I'll tell y'all a little bit about me, it may not mean anything to you. I've been to Honduras 7 times—on Mission Trips, I've been to Nicaragua, I sponsor a child with Compassion International in Honduras. . . . So don't think that we sit here and don't have compassion, care, and concern for the Latino community, because we do. We care very deeply for them. And we want you to know that we do have a job to do in law enforcement but we also are very respectful of your culture and your life in our community" (April 12, 2017, LINK meeting).

## Saviorism

Stout's comment is also emblematic of the white savior frame utilized by whites in these settings. For some—predominantly faith representatives—initial efforts to oppose the 287(g) program local efforts were not led by Latinx leaders but were spearheaded by white leaders. For local law enforcement and some local white leaders, this frame showcased their desire to rid the county of "criminals" in order to make the community safer. In Henderson County, the 2017 287(g) steering committee meeting was attended by approximately thirty white people, many of whom were also in attendance at the LINK meetings and at an additional 2017 informational meeting with Pisgah Legal Services about recent immigration enforcement measures. In Mecklenburg County, the public defender's office sued the sheriff for the use of detainers in the county jail; this lawsuit was sparked not by calls from directly impacted community members but from a recent gathering of public defenders coordinated by Gideon's Promise—a predominately white collective. Mecklenburg County public defenders noted that judges were in favor of stopping the use of detainers but that the sheriff before the 2018 election continued to work with ICE in issuing them.

Overwhelmingly, the law enforcement officers I observed in community meetings reiterated their attempts to "protect" community members from "criminals." Yet the group they are claiming to "save" or "protect" in this current moment, namely Latinx immigrants, tells a different narrative than previously expressed. And not only does this showcase law enforcement's patronizing relationship with community members, but it also does so without evidence that they are removing solely "criminals." For example, former Henderson County sheriff Charles McDonald said the following at an April 12, 2017, LINK meeting: "That's not how we do business, my ability to do the job has to do with communication with the community. . . . If anyone calls us for any service, please understand we don't care and don't ask about how you came here, we're here to make you more secure. . . . We have access to a criminal database to see who is in our community, most of y'all don't want them either."

In 2017, former Mecklenburg County sheriff Irwin Carmichael also claimed that the program kept not only the community but also his staff safe: "'In that time,' Carmichael said, 'the department has discovered it was holding undocumented immigrants who were wanted for felony child abuse, murder and possessing a weapon of mass destruction.' As a result of such arrests, Carmichael believes participating in 287(g) makes both his staff and the community safer" (Bell 2017). That same year, at a February 15 Wake County Steering Committee meeting, former sheriff of Wake County Donnie Harrison made it clear that he wanted to "get rid of" bad guys in the county: "I think that's what the president is saying and I know that's what I'm saying— if you're a bad guy regardless of who you are—I want you out of Wake County" (author's notes). ICE also utilized a savior rhetoric. Prior to the 2018 sheriff races in North Carolina, only three sheriffs claimed to not honor detainer requests from ICE, yet ICE did not highlight this noncompliance—that is, until July 23, 2018, when ICE officials made comments to the *Herald Sun* about the Orange County Sheriff's Office's decision to release an undocumented man without first notifying ICE (Lamb 2018). Allegedly, Orange County ended the practice of notifying ICE in 2017. In this instance, ICE focused on the individual's previous offense and said, "What is not in dispute is [that] the sheriff's major, [Randy Hawkins], failed to contact ICE to let us know he had an egregious criminal offender he was about to return to community" (Lamb 2018). Here in an attempt to sway public opinion, ICE paints itself as morally above the decisions of the local sheriff, particularly since this statement was not directed at the sheriff himself but was passed on to media first. Alternatively, ICE also continued to emphasize "saving" community members from collateral arrests by having 287(g) programs. This ultimatum, whereby ICE may need to conduct more field operations to find individuals they are looking for if local law enforcement does not arrest them, is an attempt to repress community-organizing efforts against these local collaborations. ICE expects people to be ignorant of their partnerships, but when people to understand them, they turn to fear mongering in their attempts to maintain control.

Local law enforcement, elected officials, and ICE officials in 287(g) counties and elsewhere utilize this rhetoric to maintain their stance on local-level implementation of federal immigration enforcement: In such statements, they maintained that they are doing a favor for the Latinx community by "saving" them from "criminals." Certain law enforcement agencies also utilized the U-Visa program, which provides a visa for victims of some crimes, as a means to "prove" that they are truly committed to issues of public safety of all community members.[2] In Durham County, both the Durham County Sheriff's Office and the Durham Police Department participate in the Faith Action Identification program and have quarterly opportunities to communicate with community members. In 2017, many of these meetings focused on the positive relationships with the Latinx and immigrant communities. Each of these agencies also stated "we are not ICE," with little to no further explanation. When pushed for rates of certifications of these types of programs and other proof of noncompliance with ICE, it becomes clear that these statements are empty promises, at a time when 44 percent of Latinxs are less likely to contact police officers because they fear deportation (Nik et al. 2013). Furthermore, "progressive" organizations that endorse or support some of these elected officials do not themselves have accountability structures in place to monitor these types of initiatives—effectively creating a no accountability feedback loop, which further contributes to a white collective amnesia.

## Non-white Participation in Collective Amnesia

Non-whites can also participate in this collective amnesia, sometimes forced to do so because of the power relations and patterns of ideological hegemony involved. As an institution, law enforcement has a long history of racism that is yet to be undone. Moreover, non-white law enforcement is often expected to police their own communities to a greater extent (Forman 2017). Although all the sheriffs in the five counties studied were white, three of the counties had Black police chiefs, who noted the pressure to appear tough on crime, which meant that they could not necessarily be lenient when it came to policies and procedures that might benefit immigrants. Often, they hid behind the "law and order" approach consistent with their white counterparts, agreeing that interventions like municipal or organizational identifications were not secure enough to be utilized as a valid form of identification in instances like routine traffic stops—the most prominent way immigrants are encountered.

Latinx community activists and Latinx staff at local nonprofits also took another trajectory altogether. Most of these community members had moved on to tackle the need for proper identification or refocused their attention toward the direct service needs of the community. The 287(g) steering committee meetings that began back in 2014 and 2015, initiated by ICE officials, revived this conversation, and the blatantly anti-immigrant and racist rhetoric characteristic of candidates up and down the ballot sparked interest from the predominantly complacent white community.

Because of their complicated relationship within the process of immigrant identification, local police chiefs were not the focus of this study, but Black police chiefs copied their white counterparts at the county level and participated in some public forums related to immigration enforcement. They also maintained skirted responsibility when it came to immigration enforcement, but for different reasons. One former police chief noted his difficult position by admitting that during his tenure, driver's licenses were no longer issued to undocumented persons. In this regard, he expressed his sympathy toward this group and then proceeded to compare his community policing efforts with the new police chief's stances. That new police chief—also a Black man— took a different stance regarding the issue of identification and emphasized he could not in good faith accept other forms of identification. He, like his counterpart in Wake County's Raleigh Police Department, expressed the same concerns about the misuse of a municipal or organizational identification program. The Raleigh police chief was dramatically impacted by remarks directed at her in a 2017 community meeting, where Latinx community members showed up to question the identification protocols of the department.

Although she did not change the department protocols, she seemed unaware of the impact that alternative forms of identification could have for those her department was meant to "protect and serve."

To further complicate this typically binary race relationship, Latinx community members exhibited a puzzling sense of ignorance. This was puzzling in the sense that community members who were involved in the movement against the program's initiation later seemed unaware of its continuation into the present day. It seemed to no longer be a frontline concern. Some were surprised to hear of the steering committee meetings since there was little open discussion of the program in the years leading up to them. Of the three counties (Wake, Henderson, and Mecklenburg) where resistance from the Latinx community was part of the initial discussions of the programs, community members in Henderson County were the least knowledgeable about the current practices of the program. Early on during my field research in 2015, I found that these individuals did not think the program still existed, although the relationships with the sheriff office was strained after the 2008 implementation of the 287(g) program. Some community groups revived a relationship with the sheriff's office during the course of this research.

Unfortunately, that relationship did not equate to the Henderson County sheriff providing relevant information about the upcoming renewal process of the 287(g) program, which must be renewed every two to three years. Instead, the sheriff did not inform these community members—many of whom work with the local Latinx-serving nonprofits—of the upcoming steering committee meeting or the renewal of the MOA with ICE. Moreover, even when groups in Wake and Mecklenburg Counties—the two counties with a continued presence of community awareness of the program—had some type of relationship with the sheriff's office, it did not result in knowing up-to-date information about the program or the status of either renewal processes and the upcoming steering committee meetings. This was showcased in Mecklenburg County when reporters who had relationships with sheriff office deputies requested more up-to-date information about detainers and deportations be included on the sheriff's office website.[3] If the office was as responsive and forthcoming as they suggested, they would be more willing to share information that could contribute to the public memory. Later that year, when these groups did become aware of the upcoming steering committee meetings, they encouraged community members to attend and even underwent their own forms of community outreach. In Cabarrus and Gaston Counties, resistance efforts remain limited and were not noted in government documents or local media.

For local Latinx community leaders, the dependence on whites who adopted the above frames and competing priorities meant that Latinxs also contribute to this collective amnesia. The issues of racial profiling, limited oversight, and targeting of immigrants with the 287(g) program are resurfacing after attacks from the federal government during the Trump administration and through the opportunity to provide public input through the 287(g) steering committee meetings.[4] Otherwise, there is little oversight of the program beyond these steering committee meetings.

## Conclusion

As previously discussed, at first, community members noted the blatant policing of their communities in the initial years of the program, but once that overt form of policing ended, more covert practices were not interrogated, contributing to the normalization of the program. The lack of transparency regarding the number of deportations and practices within the jail also bolstered this normalization. Many community members (both pro- and anti-immigrant) who may have involved themselves in the adoption process did not remain involved in accountability processes. In communities where a formal community input process was undertaken, pro-immigrant forces became frustrated with the silencing of their voices, and some settled for limited versions of immigration enforcement. By no means did these community members remove themselves entirely from related efforts, but many saw that traditional routes (appeals to city and county governments) to combat the program were exhausted. On the other hand, overtly anti-immigrant segments of these communities, albeit not entirely pleased by the level of immigration enforcement practices, were more aligned with the desires of law enforcement to enter into such agreements.

Collective amnesia of the impetus of the program (both in process and rhetoric) ensured these practices became invisible. Changes in 2015, requiring sheriff departments to host 287(g) steering committee meetings to discuss the mission and results of the program, are making the program more visible. In the initial adoption of the programs, county commissioners signed off on the MOA between the sheriff's departments and ICE. In subsequent renewal periods, only the sheriff's department signed off on the agreement, neutralizing the need and responsibility of county commissioners to be involved in the process. In recent 287(g) meetings, sheriff department representatives ignore the initial impetus for the program and deflect any anti-immigrant sentiments that previously existed by suggesting, "that was a different administration," although they are unwilling to describe any adjustments in the implementation of the program.[5] Financial benefits of the program were one of the most visible aspects of the program, yet also part of this collective amnesia, even when elected officials and law enforcement leadership were certainly aware of this.

I follow this transition to program invisibility and its transition back to visibility in the current moment to highlight how whites benefit from this program and what they ultimately chose to protect. Overwhelmingly law enforcement representatives from sheriff's offices are white, and during interactions with community members, they maintained their stance as "by the books administrators" and protectors of the community from "criminal" elements. On the other hand, white community members also distanced themselves from mostly Latinx community members who chose to engage in direct actions during the adoption phases of the program. Yet many of those white community members did not monitor the implementation practices and financial gains of the program, although they did remain involved in government input processes. In localities where community input was part of the adoption process, safeguards to ensure accountability and transparency were initially requested, yet members of those communities and local government officials did not follow up.

This invisibility also protects white economic interests and benefits majority-white communities. At the local, state, and federal levels, immigration enforcement remains at the forefront of politics. Even now, the further militarization of the border, a lack of comprehensive immigration reform, and the growth of internal immigration enforcement in new 287(g) program ensure that immigration enforcement will remain in the spotlight. But by focusing on the initial implementation of certain local law enforcement partnerships with federal immigration enforcement, we begin to see a different story of resistance and a power struggle in areas of the country where communities are attempting to maintain white dominance.

# CHAPTER 5

# Melting ICE

At the December 2015 Wake County 287(g) Steering Committee meeting, Gregorio Morales of Comite Popular Somos Raleigh stood up and said:

> Our perception of this program is completely different. Let me tell you that, the 287(g) Program didn't work from the beginning and didn't work from day 1 and HB318 is not going to work. Because we're not safer now. Do you think we are safer than before 9/11? I don't think so. It will not work. Why? Because from the beginning you decided to down the community, the Latino community under the bus. You decided not to work for the people's safety. Instead, you decided to work on behalf of the private prison shareholders. Why are so many Latinos deported for nothing? Just for a traffic violation? What is this? How do we take the racial component from this issue? Is it ethnic cleansing? Do you know that 50% of the undocumented people came by plane? We are not safe. We are less confident. We are actually scared. So that is why we are demanding Immigration and Customs Enforcement (ICE) out of North Carolina. We are demanding ICE out of every jail in North Carolina. The system is not working.

Once Gregorio made this statement at the annual 287(g) ICE enforcement partnership steering committee meeting held at the Wake County Detention Center, community members, most of whom proudly wore a black T-shirt that read "ICE Out of NC" in white letters on the front and "Stop the Hate" in red letters on the back, began shouting "ICE Out of North Carolina!" as they left the room. Most left, but four stayed, along with representatives from both Spanish-language and English-language media, to continue participating in the question-and-answer portion of the meeting, which lasted about forty minutes longer (fig. 5.1).

Over three years, I attended these meetings across the state—sometimes alone, sometimes with a familiar crowd. Sometimes people would ask where the sheriff was; sometimes I'd just ask a series of questions. And sometimes

Figure 5.1. Wake County Steering Committee meeting. Photo by Elaine Athens. Courtesy ABC News.

the questions would get shut down, like the time when the ICE southern region communications director was questioned about 2018 ICE arrests occurring in western North Carolina and instead redirected the question to underscore that the conversation was only about 287(g). In 2015, when Gregorio highlighted the 287(g) program in his own county, he also concluded his remarks by summarizing that every jail and sheriff collaborated with ICE in North Carolina and demanding ICE get out of North Carolina more broadly. He and others in the room would join together under a new effort: ICE Out of North Carolina.

Similar conversations were happening in Charlotte, North Carolina, 160 miles away. In 2015, I found myself driving down the I-85 corridor to witness a similar tension—one that would begin a three-year battle to end the 287(g) program, with repercussions not only for the Mecklenburg County Sheriff's Office but also for the entire state. This chapter tells that story, focusing on the three years (2015–18) of community pressure against local elected officials that would culminate in the termination of immigration enforcement partnerships in Wake and Mecklenburg Counties and subsequent backlash from ICE to regain the stronghold they once possessed. Grassroots activists, mainly Latinx immigrants, critical of both political parties were able to work in coalition with nonprofits while maintaining tactics and goals created outside of the state's sealed-off political realm. Pressure from these groups showed the rest of the state and even the country, that pushing back against racialized social control can lead to change.

Although previous survey research describing political participation prior to the widespread Latinx protests in 2006 argues that Latinx immigrants are less likely than U.S.-born Latinxs and other racial and ethnic groups to engage in nonpolitical activities (Verba, Schlozman, and Brady 1995; Leighly and Nagle 2013; Leal 2002; L. Martinez 2005; L. Martinez 2008), this was not the case in 2018. Furthermore, the national and state climates facilitate a limited two-political-party solution to local immigration enforcement whereby neither party has moved on progressive immigration measures. This provides a unique opportunity for nonimmigrant and immigrant grassroots activists not beholden to those parties to construct a more expansive platform for sheriff campaigns that doesn't follow those traditional political tactics like Get Out the Vote. Regardless of political affiliation of the sheriff candidates, the grassroots activists prepared to hold them accountable, shying away from the ideas that Democrats are more progressive than their Republic counterparts. In this chapter, I focus on organizations that would consider themselves part of the immigrant rights movement who decided to participate more broadly in a movement for local law enforcement accountability, as these organizations both led and participated in coalitions that they were able to navigate both within and outside the sealed-off political realm. Furthermore, the examples in this chapter show the importance of coalition building that welcomes a variety of tactics.

## Picking Up Where They Left Off: Explaining Dissent

Gregorio and other activists present at the 2015 Wake County 287(g) Steering Committee meeting had unfortunately been here before, protesting the program over the years. In Wake and Mecklenburg Counties, I found that activists, particularly Latinx immigrants, were willing to step outside the sealed-off political realm—mobilizing against both immigrant detention and mass incarceration. Therefore, opportunities for Black and brown solidarity were able to coalesce in these efforts to defeat sheriff candidates—in Wake and Mecklenburg Counties—and replace them with more "progressive" ones that would be responsive to community concerns.

Although the 287(g) steering committee meetings across the state were proposed as a place for dialogue between ICE officials and community members, over the years, this would grow more and more contentious. And the once-a-year opportunities would not prove sufficient for community members concerned about themselves and their family members. Furthermore, each county would also experience unique events that would further encourage community involvement in the annual steering committee such as statewide ICE raids in the early months of each year and the arrests of immigrant youth in 2016. In the beginning years of the steering committee meetings, most questions were directed at the ICE officials, but eventually the sheriff would become the target of the discussions. And in Mecklenburg County, this would result in more than just questions about his ICE collaboration; they would also ask about additional practices such as in-person visitations and solitary confinement at the jail.

But these efforts didn't come out of nowhere. Instead, they were consistent with what happened during the initial implementation of the programs from 2006 to 2008 where community members showed up at local government meetings to protest the program. Unfortunately, at that time, community members concerned about these programs were met with both blatantly anti-immigrant local government officials and mostly apathetic white moderates. The steering committee meetings that began in 2015 provided an opportunity for immigrant rights activists to reengage on this specific issue.

## The Build Up: Steering Committee Meetings

In the 2015 steering committee meeting in Wake County, not only were there more attendees than I had seen in other steering committee meetings I had previously attended earlier in the year, but there was also substantially more press coverage. This was also the first time I would see a community effort to publicize the event, challenging the lack of outreach on the part of the sheriff's office. In subsequent months and years, I would request the full schedule of steering committee meetings for the state but would be told that it was required only to be posted two weeks prior on the sheriff's website.

Edgar Vasquez, the 287(g) program manager at the time, needed to clear any media prior to their entering the room. He recognized me from our previous interaction at the Gaston County Steering Committee meeting earlier that year. At that meeting, I was the only non-ICE or sheriff employee, but at this one, I was joined by community members, media, and even public relations personnel from the national ICE office, an addition I would not see in subsequent meetings. In the 2017 steering committee meeting, only one community member, affiliated with a group called Si a Las Licensias; two immigration attorneys; and a representative from the North Carolina Justice Center attended. The 287(g) program manager began his presentation acknowledging that most of us in the room were more than likely familiar with this program—indicating the ICE officials' familiarity with most attendees.

In this meeting (which I recorded), the sheriff directly responded to the questions from Beckie Moriello, a local immigration attorney, in what would become a heated debate about the proper procedure of honoring ICE detainers, the transfer to ICE custody, and proper pathways to citizenship. This exchanged began civilly enough, but as Beckie began to further provide examples of her experiences where clients were being immediately transferred to ICE custody (minute 19:45), the sheriff initially responded, "Give me some names and let me check," and "Well we need to find out because I'm a believer in state charges being fulfilled—I've said that from day one." He then became visibly annoyed and began to raise his voice, saying "Now, don't twist my words" (minute 29:00). Later on in the exchanges between the sheriff and Moriello, it became clear that Sheriff Harrison did not understand the process for obtaining citizenship, particularly when he remarked, "Why don't more try to get their citizenship? Answer that question" (minute 52:30). In that exchange, the sheriff also indicated that he worked closely with the Hispanic/Latinx community, signaling to David Salazar, a community member from Si a Las Licensias who was present in the room. Then Sheriff Harrison added, "I'm willing to look into anything. I think he knows me well enough to know that I'm gonna look into it if I say I'm going to look into it." Later on in the meeting, he also added, "Now I understand where you're coming from and I understand there's a lot of people who don't like 287(g). It's a tool for me and I'm gonna keep it" (minute 52:00).

For this meeting and the one in Mecklenburg County, both in December, no statistics were provided because they had "not been cleared yet," according to ICE officials. I requested some of this information afterward—sometimes receiving it, but to my knowledge, these were not made available to the public by the sheriff or ICE afterward. In an effort to indicate transparency, the new public affairs officer, Bryan Cox, provided his direct contact information in meetings and said, "You are all good people and I trust you but y'all know there are there are also groups out there who like to do petitions and send us mass emails. . . . I am not one of those decision makers. . . . I cannot in any way have anything to do with any of that" (64:00).

It seems that 287(g) program managers get shuffled around, depending on the expected turnout at the steering committee meetings or their ability to manage those meetings. Although Edgar Vasquez would initially present at the first few 287(g) steering committee meetings I attended, he would be accompanied by a new program manager, Steve LaRocca, who would take over the meetings and operations of the program in some of the bigger counties in the six-program area: Rock Hill, South Carolina; Gaston County, North Carolina; Cabarrus County, North Carolina; Mecklenburg County, North Carolina; Henderson County, North Carolina; and Wake County, North Carolina.

In Mecklenburg County, the 2016 287(g) steering committee meeting had the most attendees of any meeting during my time in the field. As I had become accustomed to participating as the only non–law enforcement individual in meetings, I was surprised to see at this meeting that the attendees also

Table 5.1. 287(g) encounters and removal proceedings in Wake and Mecklenburg Counties, fiscal years 2016 and 2017

| | 2016 Encounters | 2016 Removals | 2016 Percentage of removals | 2017 Encounters | 2017 Removals | 2017 Percentage of removals |
|---|---|---|---|---|---|---|
| Wake County | | | | | | |
| | 1,842 | 368 | 20 | 2,055 | 130 | 6 |
| Mecklenburg County | | | | | | |
| | 1,306 | 287 | 22 | 1,241 | 100 | 8 |
| State total | | | | | | |
| | 3,551 | 777 | 22 | 3,714 | 269 | 7 |

came from more than just immigrant rights groups. Most striking was the participation of the district attorney's office and activists who participated in the Charlotte Uprising—the 2016 mobilizations in response to a police officer killing Keith Lamont Scott. The majority of the Charlotte Uprising were Black organizers in the community who came to show solidarity and to make it clear that law enforcement accountability connects racial and ethnic groups. Steve LaRocca was introduced and gave a very brief, eight-minute presentation. Questions from the audience included an emphasis on the use of the term "aliens," a request for more data since statistics were not available, and questions about the program expenses. Some of those statistics are included in table 5.1, which includes information presented at 2016 and 2017 steering committee meetings by ICE officials. These numbers reflect a shift in way ICE categorizes immigrants for removal, consistent with the Trump administration's directives to do so and subsequent priorities for deportation, which were discussed in chapter 2. Prior to this shift, this information was reported according to three priority levels. Of the five counties in the state with 287(g) partnerships, in 2016, Wake and Mecklenburg Counties made up 89 percent of the reported "encounters" and 84 percent of those removed. In 2017, they also made up 89 percent of the reported encounters and 86 percent of removals, underscoring their importance to maintaining ICE's presence within the state.[1]

As interest in the 287(g) program ramped up, local communities turned their attention to the upcoming 2018 sheriff election.

## Broadening Efforts for Black and Brown Solidarity

The 2018 sheriff elections facilitated a space for the creation of Black and brown coalitions willing to focus their attention on a hyperlocal campaigns and solutions regarding a variety of issues, some of which were met with national pushback under the Trump administration's anti-immigrant efforts. Alongside the state and federal initiatives to enhance interior immigration enforcement, the Trump administration also retaliated against immigrant right advocates. The Immigrant Rights Clinic at New York University Law School catalogued more than 1,000 incidents of retaliation (Pinto 2020). Yet these intimidation tactics did not deter community activists in Mecklenburg and Wake Counties.

In Mecklenburg County, the steering committee meetings also drew a variety of local organizations, not just immigrant rights groups. The efforts by the Charlotte Uprising, combined with the shooting of Josue Javier Diaz by an undercover police detective in 2017, encouraged groups to come together to discuss criminal justice reform issues, although mostly directed at the Charlotte Mecklenburg Police Department (Barber 2018).

In that 2016 meeting, following the trend of encouraging the sheriff to be present, the sheriff defended 287(g), and he repeated the need to identify people within the jail to community organizers. Those specific events, encouraged activists to create Comunidad Colectiva—a Latinx mostly immigrant, grassroots group based in Charlotte, North Carolina. On their website, they state, "Colectiva was created in response to the anti-immigrant rhetoric of the 2016 presidential election and the xenophobic policies of the Trump administration" (2020). I had previously met some of these activists in 2013 when coordinating state legislative efforts for in-state tuition, and over the years, they would ask me to come participate in various ways to provide additional context about the 287(g) program. In 2017, they began responding to a series of large-scale immigration raids and then turning that energy into one of the largest immigrant-related marches in Charlotte's history, with participation from approximately 8,000 people.[2] That march also encouraged community members to continuing participating in political actions like volunteering with Comunidad Colectiva and paying more attention to the upcoming sheriff election. Unfortunately, it also prompted ICE to be on the defensive, pushing harmful and fear-mongering narratives.

Later that year, many of these individuals began to show up at municipal government meetings calling for an end to the 287(g) program. They also sought to focus on the county commissioners—making the connection between sheriff department funding and the governing body that passes the sheriff's budget—but Vice Chair Jim Puckett of the county commissioners threatened this group: "I think that the presence of ICE agents might have a calming effect on anyone who is passionate, illegal and willing to cross the line of calm and deliberative public engagement" (WBTV 2017). Vice Chair Puckett wished to scare attendees from these public meetings, and unwelcoming statements like these forced organizers to shift their attention to the city council and the sheriff. ICE officials would also attend various community meetings and even created their own community forum, beyond the steering committee meeting, to try to counter the challenges to the program. And in the fall of 2017, plans to put this issue into the 2018 sheriff races began to develop. Similar plans were also brewing in Wake County—the second-longest-running 287(g) program in the state, with similarly large impacts on the immigrant community.

In Wake County, the group Familias SI, 287(g) NO formed later in September 2018 (per their Facebook page, www.facebook.com/profile.php?id=1000 64394513518), with support from the North Carolina A. Philip Randolph Education Fund, Advance Carolina, the American Civil Liberties Union (ACLU) of North Carolina, Raleigh Police Accountability Community Taskforce (PACT), Sheriffs for Trusting Communities, Comite Popular Somos Raleigh, and Comite de Accion Popular. According to their Facebook page (www.facebook .com/CPSRALEIGH), Comite Popular Somos Raleigh began their online presence in 2012 and Comite de Accion Popular (www.facebook.com/Comite-de -Accion-Popular-1793407764232468) in 2016. For the Comites, the local electoral focus on the sheriff's office would be a shift away from their efforts at the state legislature, where I would initially met many of them during the 2015 efforts to defeat House Bill 318. Although these groups had previously participated in the steering committee meetings, that focus was renewed both by additional support from the broader coalition mentioned in this paragraph and also from the defeat of Sheriff Irwin Carmichael earlier that year, an adamantly pro–287(g) program sheriff, in Mecklenburg County. The focus remained on the sheriff and did not spill over into the county commissioners—the body that has some oversight of the office and by extension the 287(g) program, although candidates for county commissioners were directly asked about local immigration efforts in 2018 voter guides produced by Democracy North Carolina and Common Cause North Carolina.[3]

## 2018: On the Campaign Trail

Early in 2018, Elon University conducted the State of Political Knowledge in North Carolina poll and found that "county sheriffs, the only local elected official included in the survey, are among the better-known politicians asked about by the Elon Poll, with nearly half of voters—46 percent—able to identify this top local law enforcement officer. Rural voters were much more likely to be able to identify their sheriff than urban voters by a 57 to 35 percent margin" (Covington 2019). Although I didn't expect to be traveling the state covering those races, I attended candidate forums in Henderson, Durham, and Wake Counties and spent time in public forums with sheriffs in Buncombe, Orange, Chatham, and Watauga Counties. I also continued participating in various community conversations to discuss the role of sheriff, particularly as it pertained to local immigration enforcement efforts. I don't recall the same levels of community interest in the 2014 sheriff elections, but it seemed to be on everyone's minds in 2018, and while many incumbents ran unopposed throughout the state, the environment in Wake and Mecklenburg Counties was distinct.

Wake County is a unique North Carolina outlier in some ways because the state legislature is also within the county limits. The immigrant rights groups in this county exhibited pressure against the sheriff and the 287(g) program for over eleven years—particularly Comite Popular Somos Raleigh, a grassroots group made up predominantly of undocumented activists. In 2015, this group along with others tied anti-immigrant legislation in House Bill 318—a bill meant to deter localities from limiting local ICE enforcement collaboration—to the local 287(g) program that operated in the jail since 2008. The incumbent sheriff, Donnie Harrison, was one of the first sheriffs in the state eager to adopt the 287(g) program (Coleman 2012). Yet, during this county's general election in November 2018, his 2018 website materials did not show bold support for the 287(g) program, as it had done in previous campaign years.

In 2018, as the end of the summer neared, a new coalition formed in Wake County: the Familias SI, 287(g) NO coalition, loosely translated as Families YES, 287(g) NO.[4] This campaign would eventually place yard signs across the county with similar messaging, such as "Vote for a Wake County Sheriff that will keep families together / *Vota para un Sheriff que luchara para Familias Unidas*" (fig. 5.2). These yard signs also asked people to visit their website to get to know the candidates (*conocer los candidatos*). This coalition ensured that the community voices impacted by the 287(g) program were front and center in the election.

When all was said and done, the ACLU would also home in on Donnie Harrison's handling of a deputy releasing a police dog from a K-9 unit on an unarmed man. Gerald Baker, the challenger, won the seat with 54.5 percent of the vote, a higher percentage than many previous challengers since Harrison had taken office in 2002. Baker referred to a previous sheriff—John H. Baker Jr., North Carolina's first Black sheriff since Reconstruction (Shaffer 2018)—

Figure 5.2. "FamiliasUnidasWake" yard sign. Photo by the author.

Figure 5.3. "Vote Out Carmichael" yard sign. Photo by the author.

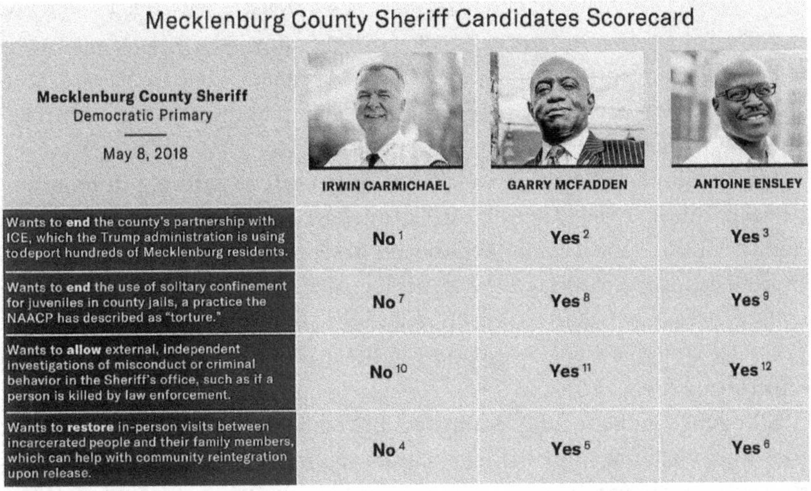

Mecklenburg County Sheriff Candidates Scorecard

| **Mecklenburg County Sheriff** Democratic Primary — May 8, 2018 | IRWIN CARMICHAEL | GARRY MCFADDEN | ANTOINE ENSLEY |
|---|---|---|---|
| Wants to **end** the county's partnership with ICE, which the Trump administration is using to deport hundreds of Mecklenburg residents. | No [1] | Yes [2] | Yes [3] |
| Wants to **end** the use of solitary confinement for juveniles in county jails, a practice the NAACP has described as "torture." | No [7] | Yes [8] | Yes [9] |
| Wants to **allow** external, independent investigations of misconduct or criminal behavior in the Sheriff's office, such as if a person is killed by law enforcement. | No [10] | Yes [11] | Yes [12] |
| Wants to **restore** in-person visits between incarcerated people and their family members, which can help with community reintegration upon release. | No [4] | Yes [5] | Yes [6] |

Figure 5.4. ACLU and Action NC scorecard for Mecklenburg County sheriff candidates. ACLU and Action NC, https://www.peoplepower.org/mecklenburg.

as his influence and guide. Donnie Harrison's campaign had outspent Baker's, but it was not enough to counter the negative publicity from the 287(g) program and the K-9 incident.

In that year, similar efforts targeted the Mecklenburg County sheriff, Irwin Carmichael, but with an even stronger message: Vote Out Carmichael. At first, the public campaign to intervene in the Mecklenburg County sheriff's race did not extend beyond the focus on the sheriff's collaboration with ICE. That slowly changed, as activists focused on an electoral strategy to not only end the 287(g) program but also end the tenure of a sheriff reluctant to be transparent and accountable to a variety of community concerns. One immigrant-led group in particular took the lead on changing the public narrative about the immigration enforcement partnership. Comunidad Colectiva brought the 287(g) program to the forefront of the Mecklenburg sheriff race. Activists Oliver Merino and Stefania Arteaga attended fundraisers for candidates to question their platforms, positioned "No 287(g), Vote out Carmichael" signs around town (fig. 5.3), and canvassed within the Latinx community to bring awareness about the local immigration enforcement partnership.

Although other contentious issues including the use of youth solitary confinement, independent oversight, and in-person visitations accompanied the sheriff election (see fig. 5.4), Comunidad Colectiva's actions garnered a great deal of media and community attention, even forcing some community members to respond by printing their own signs explaining why the 287(g) program was beneficial to their communities.[5] This was paired with canvassing efforts by Action NC and ACLU of North Carolina / ACLU-National. By the end of the primary in May 2018, the ACLU had spent $175,000 in the race (Morrill and Gordon 2018) as part of an intentional national effort to "reinvent" itself (Wallace-Wells 2018).

But Comunidad Colectiva wasn't the only party embarking in nontraditional political tactics. Then sheriff Carmichael also resorted to going on *Fox and Friends* to appeal to the Republican base, even though he was running in the Democratic primary. His main focus? Immigration, in hopes that a conservative base would support him and the continuation of the 287(g) program. He would also receive support in the media from ICE. But even those efforts were futile.

Bilingual candidate forums were few and far between, but in Wake County, they were encouraged by the local Latinx-serving organization, though getting both sheriff candidates to attend became a challenge, particularly given the focus on the 287(g) program. In October, in an unusual setup, a forum took place at the Alamo Drafthouse in conjunction with Raleigh PACT, El Pueblo, Zeta Phi Beta Sorority, Inc., North Carolina Asian Americans Together, and Delta Sigma Theta Sorority (Morales 2018). At this particular candidate forum, I was given a shirt from the Familias SI, 287(g) NO coalition. Printed on it was their campaign slogan and a luchador—an image of a wrestler popular in Mexican culture. Sheriff Donnie Harrison tried to pinpoint challenger Gerald Baker's misunderstanding of the 287(g) program; and after the forum, community members in attendance informally remarked on Baker's unfamiliarity with the program. In his address, Baker reiterated his desire to end the 287(g) program. Afterward, two community groups, Comite de Accion Popular and Comite Popular Somos Raleigh, jointly reiterated that they would not endorse either candidate: "Estamos aquí, para que los programas como el 287g no continúen. No estamos ni a favor ni en contra de algún candidato, simplemente que este tipo de programas dejen de estar en nuestras comunidades separando a nuestras familias [We are here so that programs like 287(g) do not continue. We are not here in favor or against either candidate, simply that this type of program is no longer in our communities separating our families]."

Later that month, I attended a nonpartisan storytelling event by the same coalition, where Wake community members would "tell their stories about interactions with the Wake County Sheriff's Office, including the effect of the 287(g) program" (Familias SI, 287[g] NO Event October 28, 2018, Facebook event description 2019). Gerald Baker also attended the event. Community members shared their stories about interacting with the sheriff's office, and one participant, Yolanda Zavala, described her experience of her son's deportation when the 287(g) program first began. Over the years, I have heard her tell that story a few times, yet she—like many of the women leading these efforts—continues to fight for the end to these types of partnerships. These women—Yolanda Zavala, Martha Hernandez, and Griselda Alonso—were featured in a 2019 piece by the ACLU of North Carolina titled "We Deserve to Live without Fear" (Mora 2019), a sentiment they reiterated and expanded upon by saying, "We took the risk when we crossed the border." Over the years, they have also repeated these things to me countless times when I have asked them if they fear any backlash for their community activism.

## Spillover Effects and Changing the Narrative

In counties other than Wake and Mecklenburg and across the state more generally, sheriff collaboration with ICE became an important issue, even for counties without 287(g) programs (Powers 2018). Two of these counties—Alamance and Durham—can be considered the extremes of this discussion. On the one hand, no challenger would face pro-287(g) sheriff Terry Johnson in Alamance County, and in Durham County, challenger Clarence Birkhead would echo many of the reforms proposed by community members. The interest in ICE collaboration also reflects the growing statewide coalition efforts forming to target this form of racialized social control. Even when sheriffs did not have 287(g) programs, community members engaged in efforts to better understand ICE collaboration in their own backyards.

In Alamance County, North Carolina—which previously operated with a 287(g) program, up until 2012, when the Department of Justice launched an investigation into its implementation—Sheriff Terry Johnson was also up for reelection, but he did not face a challenger, perhaps indicating an unwillingness to challenge the status quo. That did not stop community members from Down Home North Carolina and Siembra North Carolina from drawing attention to the possibilities of the reinstatement of a 287(g) program and the fear that some immigrants still felt. These organizations used contentious tactics such as street theater and protests not seen in the county since the adoption of the program back in 2008. They too joined in the 2018 Chinga La Migra tour previously mentioned in chapter 3 meant to bring awareness about immigration enforcement across the country. These organizations quickly adjusted their strategy to include targeting and supporting county commissioners also up for election in November 2018. While county commissioners do not have full oversight of the sheriff's office, they do approve the sheriff's budget and can make recommendations to the office. Understanding the connection between the sheriff's office and county commissioners was growing across the state, but in Durham County, this was old news.

In 2012, the Inside-Outside Alliance, a group of people trying to support the struggles of those inside (or formerly inside) Durham County jail, was formed, and in 2017, they began weekly protests outside of the Durham County Detention Center in downtown Durham, North Carolina. From 2014 to 2017, a variety of efforts concerning law enforcement misconduct, accountability, and transparency targeted both the Durham Police Department and the Durham Sheriff's Office, particularly the death of Chuy Huerta in police custody in 2013 and the deaths of Matthew McCain and Dennis McMurray at the Durham County Jail in 2016.

Throughout the 2018 sheriff election in Durham County, media attention proved instrumental for grassroots organizers. During and prior to the election, criticism of the sheriff came from a variety of collectives, many of whom were willing to risk arrest to draw attention to the issues of jail deaths, video visitations, and detainer requests. These groups, Alerta Migratoria and the Inside-Outside Alliance, were joined by the Decriminalize Durham campaign coordinated by Durham 4 All, among others.

The incumbent sheriff, Mike Andrews, ran as a Democrat and had received endorsements from various progressive organizations in his 2014 electoral campaign .[6] Unfortunately, there were no accountability measures once he was elected. During his tenure, incidents that prompted requests for accountability included multiple jail deaths, a lack of transparency with the community, and conflicting information about ICE collaboration. I was wrapping up my doctoral program in Durham during this election and had become familiar with these issues the previous year in my role with the City of Durham's Human Relations Commission and while completing public records requests for local community groups. In some respects, 2018's newly elected sheriff, Sheriff Birkhead, has gone the furthest in efforts of local accountability by creating a community advisory board (Birkhead 2019). But racialized social control extends beyond a sheriff's collaboration with immigration enforcement meaning that there are ample opportunities for accountability as long as the sheriff's office exists.

## Election Day 2018

In communicating with local activists during the 2018 sheriff elections, I sensed similar hopes and investment in the local electoral cycle. In May, and again in November 2018, I found myself celebrating not the win of a sheriff challenger in Mecklenburg and Wake, the two counties responsible for deporting the majority of individuals within the state, but the community efforts that put an end to unchecked political power and brought back accountability in the sheriff's office.

Figure 5.5. Front page of *HOLA News.* Courtesy *HOLA News.*

Local efforts in Mecklenburg County paid off early. That celebration began in May 2018, when Gary McFadden won the democratic primary with 52 percent of the vote in Mecklenburg County, encouraging others across the state who still had a whole summer of campaigning until their respective general elections. The Democratic incumbent in that race was last elected in 2014, but he had served in the office for thirty-two years. No Republicans was running against the Democrats, meaning that Sheriff McFadden would have a head start on preparing for his swearing-in ceremony in December 2018. During that period, he faced harsh criticism (local, state, and federal), and ICE actively wanted to meet him to discuss the 287(g) program.

On election day itself, I wasn't able to attend a Mecklenburg County watch party hosted by local activists in Charlotte, but I watched the results come in and waited for the live reactions from the organizers I continue to stay in touch with. The caption "Dijieron No al 287(g)" (which translates to "They Said No to 287[g]") accompanied a picture of the cofounders of Comunidad Colectiva at an election watch party as they celebrated the end of Carmichael's term as sheriff (fig. 5.5). Local Spanish-media representatives were present at their watch party and captured their reactions. A few months later, one of those cofounders, Stefania Arteaga, would also be featured in various news outlets while cutting a cake with the sheriff-elect to signify the end of the 287(g) program.

While I couldn't be in Charlotte on November 7, 2018, I planned to go to two watch parties—one in Wake County and one in Durham County (hosted by the People's Alliance). Early polls on election day showed Gerald Baker leading Wake County's race, a surprise to many, given the minimal campaign he had run against a popular incumbent (Nichanian 2018). Although Familias SI, 287(g) NO in Wake County supported the Gerald Baker campaign, after the celebration, they would push for the new sheriff to remain accountable to these constituents, meaning that the avenues for conversation were not as consistent as those witnessed in Mecklenburg County.

In a press conference in front of the Wake County Courthouse days after Gerald Baker defeated Donnie Harrison, I was able to witness members of the Familias SI, 287(g) NO coalition describe their purpose (McDonald 2018).[7] Maria Jimenez, from Comite de Accion Popular, said, "You kiss and hug your family because you don't know if it's the last kiss you're going to give them." "What motivated us," said Griselda Alonso from Comite Popular Somos Raleigh, "was this system that has been separating our families." And Ivanna Gonzales, a board member of the campaign, told the people assembled, "But this is just the beginning. We are here to make sure change happens within. Baker needs our support. But we need to make sure he keeps his promise to make sure everything is done."

The *Raleigh News and Observer* ran the headline "Activists Vow to Hold New Wake Sheriff Accountable on Promise to End Immigration Program" (McDonald 2018), which demonstrates the challenge with ensuring that policy change occurs once a person is elected. At the press conference were also representatives from Raleigh PACT, ACLU of North Carolina, Advance Carolina, and the A. Philip Randolph Education Fund. This event also became an opportunity to feature the recent detention of a man—Camilo Coronilla—caught up in the interim period of the sheriff office changes to the 287(g) program.

However, not everyone was celebrating these "progressive" sheriffs. Some negative responses came immediately from future employees. Less discussed in the public is the fact that a newly elected sheriff also brings in new administrative staff. Although not reported on for the numerous offices that saw Black sheriffs elected, it's easy to imagine that institutions with a legacy of upholding white supremacy (regardless of political party affiliation), might not be ready for a shift to new leadership.[8] In certain circumstances, this was reported as an issue of loyalty, resulting in a "bloodletting" (aka mass firings) (Yost 2018). This was more public in Guilford County, where the *Rhino Times* reported the back-and-forth between the former sheriff B. J. Barnes and the sheriff-elect at the time, Danny Rogers. In some races, the blessing of the former sheriff should have allowed for an easy transition into the office, yet some of these newly elected sheriffs faced less than supportive circumstances, on top of negative media reporting orchestrated by ICE enforcement that continued into the following years. For example, ICE created a website (no longer live) specifically for North Carolina to shame the newly elected sheriffs' efforts to end collaboration (Billman 2019). Black sheriffs were elected in the seven largest counties in North Carolina, including the election of the first Black female sheriff in the state's history (Killian 2018).

## 2019 Backlash and the "New Normal"

As I indicated earlier, these "wins," particularly for the immigrant community, would be met with additional scrutiny from ICE, the attorney general, and the North Carolina Sheriffs' Association, among others. Threats from these bodies continued even once the candidates won their respective campaigns. ICE director Sean Gallagher would continue this dynamic in a press conference in early February 2019, where he suggested that targeted enforcement operations would become the new normal as a result of these sheriffs' end to ICE collaboration. Although this was mainly directed at Wake and Mecklenburg Counties, sheriffs in Forsyth, Buncombe, Durham, and Guilford Counties also took some steps in limiting cooperation. Yet, prior to this, racial profiling and sending information about a person's legal status was just a "normal" part of daily life if someone encountered local law enforcement. The fear and anxiety people of color feel when they encounter local law enforcement is also a normal part of people's lives, but it should never be normalized. Instead, we should work toward a new normal where this does not occur, a new normal where local agencies aren't threated because they choose to end voluntary ICE partnerships.

Like many of those community members who perhaps regained some sense of hope on Election Day 2018, targeted ICE operations in February came as a bombshell to me and the organizers who fought to bring an end to sheriff collaboration with ICE. On February 13, 2019, I woke up to alerts that ICE was in my hometown. The weekend before, I had spent time driving around and verifying whether or not ICE was in Durham, North Carolina, my previous home for the past ten years. And when I returned to my home in Boone on a Sunday night, I reflected on the community's ability to respond to targeted ICE enforcement and the sheriff's current collaboration with ICE. As I was relatively new to Boone, I knew there was a local group called the Immigrant Justice Coalition that could spring into action if needed.

I also spent some time going through videos and posts from various community organizations documenting the ICE presence in their communities. I was hoping to find some patterns. One thing that I couldn't shake from the press conference in early February was that ICE was trying to send a message, and not just through the media. I watched a video of ICE stopping a van on the side of the road in Charlotte, North Carolina, that was uploaded by Comunidad Colectiva. And when I looked at the video, I realized that the officer requesting information from the driver was assistant field office director Robert J. Alfrieri, who let the driver go without further questions when he saw the driver recording the interaction. Most of the time when I write about ICE officials, I'm not typically writing about the actual managers of the organization. I'm writing about those folks who are based in jails. So seeing this high-level employee participating in these recent arrests and the threats from the press conference tells me that ICE leadership really had a stake in responding to the "loss" of at two 287(g) programs in counties with large immigrant communities and the entities they have traditionally depended on to remove the majority of immigrants they have detained in North Carolina. In March, a month after the targeted enforcement operations, House Bill 370, Sheriffs to Cooperate with ICE would be introduced in the state legislature, mirroring Senate Bill 4 in Texas—a legislative response to the ending of a local 287(g) program. In response to community wins, ICE officials worked with senators and Sheriff Sam Page from Rockingham County to construct the language of the proposal.

## Conclusion

Throughout 2019, I helped convene the House Bill 370 Coalition, formed to counter the Sheriffs to Cooperate with ICE Bill. Various business, faith, non-profit, and grassroots groups came together to form a strategy to counter this proposed legislation, and the newly elected sheriffs from across the state also came to defend themselves against more conservative sheriffs and lawmakers who called them "sanctuary sheriffs." As I write this book, I have had the pleasure to visit the groups that previously worked on these campaigns. Many of them joined in for a national convening in 2020 to bring together groups working on sheriff elections across the country in a push to draw much-needed attention to the role of sheriffs.

There are still many questions about "progressive" sheriffs. In 2020, the presidential election received much attention, but more importantly in North Carolina, all eyes were on Governor Cooper, who chose to veto House Bill 370. In other places across the country, bail reforms and the end to ICE partnerships have resulted in a decrease in the jail population, forcing a reimagination of jails (Alsous 2019). In North Carolina, only Durham has both a progressive district attorney and a progressive sheriff, so perhaps similar changes could result in other parts of the state. During my time on the City of Durham's Human Relations Commission, we created recommendations for the jail, prompted by many of the groups previously mentioned. Some of those recommendations included having a sheriff accountability board, keeping in-person visitation, and ending the use of ICE detainers.

All those recommendations have since been followed by Sheriff Birkhead, but these were just a few of the community-proposed recommendations (Durham Human Relations Commission 2017). Moreover, no one saw COVID-19 coming—a pandemic that continues to highlight the evils of mass incarceration. Yet many questions remain regarding immigration enforcement: Is there a possibility for a statewide reform when it comes to ICE partnerships? In what ways will ICE adjust to these changes? And are initiatives in other states predictive of what's to come, such as the newly introduced Warrant Service Officer program in Florida? The concluding chapter dives into these questions. As these localities move to alter local-level participation, ICE is also shifting—to spread additional fear into communities by doubling down in some arenas. But I have hope that our communities are coming together to push for community-based strategies to address these concerns while making hidden practices more visible.

# CHAPTER 6

# *La migra, la policia, la misma porqueria* (Ice, the Police, the Same Crap)

OPPORTUNITIES AND CHALLENGES FROM
THE 2018 JUSTICE ELECTION

The end to the 287(g) programs described in chapter 5 was both an opportunity and a challenge for many of the crimmigration bodies—sheriff's offices, county commissions, and so on—described in chapter 2. For starters, the ending of the 287(g) programs not only paved the way for discussions elsewhere throughout the state, but they also did so across the country. Yet these advances also ignited negative reactions from various officials. While many communities scrutinized sheriffs during this election, that scrutiny also fanned out to include other criminal-legal actors that make up the touch points (to use Immigration and Customs Enforcement [ICE] terminology) or what Spanish-speaking communities call the *poli-migra*. While many people cannot differentiate what criminal-legal entity is responsible for what, the 2018 election also encouraged political organizations to educate people about these down-ballot, or local, races.

The "Justice Election"—a statewide initiative to focus on state and local races occurring in 2018 that included sheriffs, district attorneys, district court judges, and North Carolina Supreme Court seats—in North Carolina focused on down-ballot races, forcing candidates to respond to a variety of criminal justice reform issues. For example, candidates for district attorney were asked how they would address prosecution of nonviolent offenses like disruptive public assembles and marijuana possession, how they would minimize mass incarceration, how they would address bail issues, and their views on special prosecutors to investigate and prosecute police misconduct or police killing a civilian (2018 Guide to Voting for Wake County). Candidates for sheriff were asked how they would keep incarcerated individuals safe and connected to family members and community, what they believe the appropriate level of collaboration between ICE and the sheriff's office was, whether cities and counties should have the ability to establish community/civilian oversight boards with subpoena power, and how they would minimize racial bias in stops and searchers (2018 Guide to Voting for Wake County).

Immigration enforcement practices became central to key races as well, and in the three largest counties—Wake, Durham, and Mecklenburg, candidates won who committed to end immigration detainer usage, and two ended their county's 287(g) programs. Furthermore, sheriff elections in 2018 forced ICE to make some distinctions among its programs, particularly in localities where candidates included noncompliance with ICE as part of their platform. Unfortunately, as we have seen, ICE also took this opportunity to further threaten and demonize the Latinx immigrant community. Moreover, ICE and sheriffs who support collaboration emphasized the possibility of "collateral" arrests by ICE officials out in the field (DeGrave 2018; Feldblum 2018).

The 2018 sheriff elections in North Carolina presented a unique opportunity for local immigration enforcement practices to be front and center, particularly in the largest counties in North Carolina. After I had spent three years diving into this information about sheriffs, the election also became an opportunity for me to contribute directly to these local efforts. Prior to this, I had given a few related presentations or provided relevant information to community groups who were unable to access the information themselves. But the Justice Election propelled us into new arenas. For some of these groups, they now have extensive relationships with the newly elected sheriffs, while others—like Comite Popular Somos Raleigh and Comite de Accion Popular described in chapter 5—did not receive a welcome reception from the sheriff's office. In places where sheriffs did not face substantive challengers in 2018, some community organizers continue to push forward, most notably in Orange and Alamance Counties, where they sought to challenge other types of local law enforcement partnerships with ICE beyond 287(g) program participation. Although the Justice Election provided an opportunity for interests to intersect, an electoral win is only one measure of success. What happens next is another challenge and an opportunity to break through the sealed-off political realm.

## Building an Intersectional, Multi-issue Approach

While national elections are very important, local elections and the officials that win them impact us in a more direct way. But often we are not engaged by those who are running for these offices, and this is even more true for certain communities like Black and brown working-class people. Moreover, we are the ones who face the brunt of local policies made without our perspectives.

But there comes a time when we say enough is enough and push to make our presence known in political spheres that neglect us. Francesca Polletta (2002) challenges readers to reconsider the cultural models on which movements have depended to enact social change and their commitments to one another. Whereas mainstream state and national partners with local chapters were dependent on their voter mobilization tactics, grassroots group participants—many unable to vote—were not constrained by this. Instead, these coalitions were able to embrace a more participatory democracy model "where conventional qualifications were no indicator of people's capacities for political leadership" (Polletta 2002, 205).

The social movement organizations described in this book often took direction from directly impacted individuals who did not fit the traditional political leadership model. Some political analysts suggest that this is necessary, particularly during a time when the Democratic Party at the national level is attempting to reinvent itself and incorporate more youth and people of color. Whereas individual groups may have worked on a specific policy or issue areas for an extended amount of time prior to these elections, in each county, local coalitions adopted shared platforms and shared opportunities to interrogate candidates through candidate forums, scorecards, and the like. They also engaged in actions that took people by surprise and did not adhere to what Kalir and Wissink would call legitimate actions (2016, 46). Calling out candidates in public forums and events challenged the expectations that campaigns should be civil discourses. Moreover, these activists showed people that when policies like 287(g) programs and incarceration more broadly are dehumanizing, there should be little expectation of civil responses. While Black and brown activists took one approach; progressive whites were also participating but with different motives.

In 2018, "Flip NC!" became a rallying cry for many, mostly newly activated whites to encourage the restoration of a Democratic-controlled North Carolina state legislature. In 2018, the Republican Party held a supermajority in the state and continued to strip powers from the Democratic governor. For some groups, electing Democrats regardless of the candidate's history was a priority. As previously mentioned, the dominance of the Republican Party in some parts of the state made it possible for Democratic candidates to be elected without much scrutiny. Two incidents exemplify this lack of accountability for Democratic candidates from 2014 to 2018. First, Cathy von Hassel-Davies, a Democratic candidate for the North Carolina State House in an Alamance County district, dropped out of the race in late July 2018 after anti-immigrant comments from an old blog post surfaced. Initially the North Carolina Democratic Party did not make a statement, but they eventually distanced themselves from her (Specht 2018). The Hispanic-American Caucus also met with her and asked her to step down. Second, in the fall of 2018, the Durham People's Alliance (PA)—a self-proclaimed progressive grassroots organizations in Durham, North Carolina, with a mission to "elect progressive people to office and hold them accountable 365 days a year"—had to come to terms with their 2014 endorsement of then sheriff Mike Andrews (People's Alliance 2014). The PA's membership did not endorse him again for sheriff; instead, community organizers brought up the litany of grievances against him, highlighting the issues with the jail over the course of his four years in office—all of which the PA did not seem to openly want to discuss on their own. In Durham, this organization is known to be influential in every election, yet they struggled to create accountability systems for those they elected.

More largely, because the local governments in Mecklenburg and Durham Counties are Democrat controlled, the assumption existed that sheriffs in these counties act in ways consistent with Democratic values. However, two things were true about sheriffs: they reflect the broader lack of knowledge of local ICE partnerships—both Republican and Democrat sheriffs participate in these collaborations—and they typically do not run enforcement-light campaigns.

However, in 2018, a handful of grassroots activists stepped out of this partisan politics conversation to challenge both the tactics utilized during these races and to broaden the platforms that sheriff-elects will adopt once they enter office. In Wake County, activists focused on keeping families together, jail deaths, and poorly handled use of force. In Durham County, they wanted an end to the sheriff's partnership with ICE, an end to money bail, more transparency and accessibility, and keeping people out of jail (Indy Staff 2018). Finally, in Mecklenburg County, activists worked for in-person visitations and an end to both solitary confinement and the sheriff's partnership with ICE. People became more aware of the power of the sheriff, and communities began recognizing their responsibility to keep the office accountable. While the election may have various ripple effects, my hope is that communities will understand that an end to ICE enforcement is just one example of holding sheriffs accountable.

## 2018 Shifts in Collaboration

ICE enforcement was at the forefront of the 2018 election cycle— encouraging sheriffs to make changes in their policies. Some "progressive" detainer policies make exceptions for individuals who are charged or convicted with more sever crimes while others are not. In 2019, none of the four sheriffs—of Buncombe, Mecklenburg, Durham, and Wake Counties—who claimed to not honor detainers had a formally written policy for this. Without the written policies, our understanding of internal workings of sheriff's offices is limited, obscuring our understanding of whom they deem suitable for deportation at the local level. Furthermore, ICE's definition of *criminal* stood in contrast to that of some of the sheriff's offices. National groups like TRAC who request data from the federal government pertaining to criminal records and ICE apprehension have found it challenging to obtain this information in recent years, and the Trump administration's return to Secure Communities suggested there is great uncertainty about a person's likelihood of being arrested and turned over to ICE for any offense.

During this time, the 287(g) program and detainer usage became front and center in the Mecklenburg County sheriff's race. Two of the three Democratic candidates agreed to end the 287(g) program, while the third, the incumbent, maintained his desire to keep the program. Sheriff Carmichael echoed the warnings made by ICE officials in the 287(g) steering committee in Henderson County. A small community group, Comunidad Colectiva, put pressure on all these candidates to discuss the program during a variety of public events and led the local campaign against the 287(g) program that had deported 15,000 immigrants over a ten-year period. Immediately after Carmichael lost (WSOC-TV 2018) to Gary McFadden, ICE put out a statement again warning how the end of the program would affect ICE operations locally.

Two hours away, although with no 287(g) program, detainer usage also became an important issue in the Durham County sheriff's race. After years of questioning the incumbent, Mike Andrews, about his collaboration with ICE, a challenger promised a different way forward—both more transparent and willing to end collaboration with ICE. Clarence Birkhead overwhelmingly won the election, also provoking a response from ICE officials (Blythe 2018). Communities across the state were challenging the status quo by bringing ICE collaboration out of a collective amnesia. While the bigger counties in the state were openly grappling with ICE collaboration and their county's purposely hidden role in it, smaller localities were also grappling with the collaboration, albeit without drawing much attention. It was clear that these bigger counties were instrumental in ICE's plan to have collaborative sheriffs positioned in strategic places across the state. ICE knew they could count on these bigger counties to arrest and then turn over immigrants for deportation. Some of that changed in 2018, prompting ICE to retaliate and respond.

## 2019 ICE Response and State Representatives

On March 14, 2019, the Require Sheriff Cooperation with ICE Bill was introduced by House representatives Destin Hall (Caldwell), Brendon Jones (Columbus/Robeson), Jason Saine (Lincoln), and Carson Smith (Columbus/ Pender). In an interview for *Spectrum News*, Representative Destin Hall later described ICE contacting him to assist in introducing the bill (Capital Tonight Staff 2019). According to Hall, "There is a small number of sheriffs who represent our largest counties who have decided to not even cooperate, and in many cases, not even communicate with ICE or our federal immigration authorities as it relates to illegal immigrants who have been charged with a crime. . . . I wouldn't have known that but for working with ICE on this bill, getting some direction from them" (4:30). In this exchange, Representative Hall addressed the issue of 287(g), stating it has nothing to do with his bill. Although he says that these "sanctuary" sheriffs were not communicating with ICE, he neglected to describe the biometric screening, including fingerprints, required by state law. His comments were meant to convince listeners that sheriffs were letting "criminals" walk free. Furthermore, this instance shows that ICE is willing to be explicit in their attempts—wanting all sheriffs to work with them. These representatives were sympathetic to ICE and eager to put a law together to further ICE reach throughout the state.

During the hearing in the Rules, Calendar, and Operations Committee in early April 2019, various sheriffs who ran on commitments to end certain ICE partnerships spoke out against the proposed legislation and defended themselves against the label of being a "sanctuary sheriff." They emphasized their dedication to protecting all community members and their history of doing so prior to their election wins in 2018. One sheriff, Sam Page of Rockingham County, spoke for the proposed legislation. The North Carolina Sheriffs' Association general counsel also requested that the committee table the proposed legislation until the Sheriffs' Association could convene to discuss these matters further. General Counsel Edmond Caldwell noted that there was limited communication between the bill sponsors and the Sheriffs' Association prior to that moment.

Within the next two days, the Sheriffs' Association would meet and draft a statement against the legislation (Willets 2019). House representatives received that statement while other legislation came to the House floor, causing leadership to caucus for a brief time before ultimately coming back for the final vote. Voting fell along party lines, and the legislation went to the Senate. That original proposed legislation would require sheriffs and jails to determine the immigration of every person arrested and to comply with immigration detainer requests. Furthermore, if localities were thought to be out of compliance with this law, a private citizen could file a complaint against them, which could result in penalties of up to $1,500 per day.

After a few weeks, the North Carolina Sheriffs' Association met again to discuss a "compromise." The result? Various amendments to the original version of the proposed legislation while the association voted to completely gut the text and propose new measures. These amendments required jails to determine the immigration status of every person and to notify ICE if that person is not a legal resident or citizen and detailed that if ICE responds by issuing a detainer request, sheriffs must bring the person in front of a judicial official and then that official can decide to issue an order to hold that person for ninety-six hours, which is longer than the federal regulation that allows for up to forty-eight hours retention based on an ICE detainer. This so-called compromise legislation continued into the second part of the legislative session yet did not come back up for a vote in 2020. Unfortunately, some sheriffs across the state were still busy ushering in a new version of the 287(g) program and poorly managing COVID-19 outbreaks. While the state legislature was not willing to mandate sheriffs collaboration with ICE, some sheriffs looked toward the 2020 election for a chance to campaign for federal-level changes.

## 2020 Elections and the New 287(g)

While spearheading the efforts to force every sheriff in North Carolina to collaborate with ICE, in 2019, Sheriff Sam Page was also busy becoming the first North Carolina sheriff to sign on to the Warrant Service Officer Program, a newly constructed version of the 287(g) program (aka 287[g] lite). This new version is supposed to have a much more limited scope where delegated local officers are authorized to execute ICE administrative warrants only within the jail (ILRC 2019). Sheriff Sam Page was the first of seven to very quietly sign on to the program. As of October 2020, seventy-four law enforcement agencies in eleven states had adopted this newer version of the program, almost outnumbering the "older" jail enforcement model. In 2020, some politicians who voted against the House Bill 370 "compromise" in 2019 were attacked in their reelection campaigns, and although 472 administrative changes were made by the Trump administration that "dismantled and reconstructed many elements of the U.S. immigration system" (Bolter, Israel, and Pierce 2022), there is limited hope that the Biden/Harris administration will dramatically repair it.

Early in the election cycle, Biden's immigration platform missed the mark.

A scorecard from the Refugee and Immigrant Center for Education and Legal Services (RAICES) compared various immigration policies proposed by then presidential hopefuls Biden, Sanders, and Trump ("Guest Contributor" 2020). This scorecard grouped immigration policies into three substantive areas: Equality and Inclusion for All People, Build Bridges Not Walls, and We Are Here Because You Were There. Of that first section, decoupling federal immigration enforcement and local law enforcement is not a priority for the Biden administration, although Biden did immediately reverse some of Trump's policies like the travel ban and temporarily halting the construction of the border wall.

Overall, Biden received a C+ on this scorecard, and even Bernie Sanders did not receive an A, indicating how challenging it is to hope for substantive immigration policies in this country.

Related to the third section of the score card, the Biden administration laid out some proposed policies during the 2020 campaign meant to address the root causes of migration. Yet in 2021 a series of events shows the limited progress on this front. In June 2021, Vice President Kamala Harris traveled to Central America to address concerns about migration, telling migrants not to come to the United States. While the administration has coordinated some private investments in Central American countries (Jaffe 2021), they have also expanded the Remain in Mexico policy that requires that asylum seekers await their asylum hearings in Mexico—mostly in encampments—before entering the United States (Montoya-Galvez 2022). This policy began under the Trump administration, and the Biden administration has attempted to roll it back, but a federal appeals court determined the first attempt was unlawful (Montoya-Galvez 2022). And Central Americans aren't the only ones caught up in this program. In September 2021, infamous pictures of U.S. Border Patrol agents on horseback attempting to stop Haitian migrants went viral. These migrants are some of the estimated 15,000 Haitians who made it through Mexico into Texas, while almost 130,000 migrants applied for protections in Mexico (Kahn 2021). But those aren't the only immigration issues facing the Biden administration.

Unsurprisingly, on January 20, 2022, secretary of homeland security Alejandro N. Mayorkas—the first Latinx head of the department—told the Conference of Mayors that ICE, "the agency of today and what it is focused upon, and what it is doing, is not the agency of the past." In addition, he talked about a renewed effort to encourage localities to participate with ICE while also recognizing the distrust that led many mayors to adopt sanctuary city policies in the first place: "And so, I will be coming to you and asking you to reconsider your position of noncooperation and see how we can work together. And I may not succeed initially in a wholesale reversal of your position, but I am willing to work in increments with you because the public's safety, the public's well-being, for which we are all charged, is I think at issue" (Mayorkas 2022). While many immigrant rights activists were shocked by the secretary's remarks, others see hope in holding their local- and state-level officials accountable.

How do accountability structures develop and persist? Will these social movement organizations not dependent on election cycles be more equipped to maintain the loose coalitions and pressure points that existed during the election cycle? Where does the continuum end, and how do researchers and community activists alike identify campaign targets? These are some of the central questions in the book and the most relevant to organizing today. By tracing the normalization of crimmigration—the criminalization of immigration—in counties throughout North Carolina, I sought to uncover the processes and lack of accountability systems that allow for unchecked power in the sheriff's office when it comes to immigration enforcement matters. Yet even diving into this one program only begins to scratch the surface of ICE collaboration and state efforts to circumvent local "welcoming" and "sanctuary" policies.

At the national level, I have yet to hear calls for the end of communication between ICE and probation offices and the other entryways into the criminal-legal system detailed in chapter 2. This demonstrates the complicated nature of the frames used by criminal-legal actors and nonprofit organizations. Even calls to Abolish ICE solely focus our efforts on pushing back against the criminalization of immigrants rather than forcing us to consider what an # AbolishPrisons, Police, and ICE framing and scope would encompass. One group—Detention Watch Network—has taken an innovative approach to this question in their newly developed online resource "Ending Immigrant Detention: Abolitionist Steps vs. Reformist Reforms" (2022). This approach is borrowed from the efforts of the group Critical Resistance, who in 2020 offered the one-page guides "Reformist Reforms vs. Abolitionist Steps in Policing" and "Reformist Reforms vs. Abolitionist Steps to End Imprisonment." In those two resources, Critical Resistance uses a matrix to show whether a criminal-legal policy is reformist—meaning it "continues or expands the reach" of the carceral state—or abolitionist—meaning it "chips away and reduces its overall impact" (Critical Resistance 2020a). With those parameters in mind, the Detention Watch Network's "Ending Immigrant Detention" asks similar questions of proposed policies at the local, state, and federal levels:

- Does this reduce the scale of detention and surveillance?
- Does this chip away at the current system without creating new harms or helping some people at the expense of others?
- Does this provide relief to people who could be or are currently detained or under surveillance?

Piecemeal reforms will continue to just remix policies that will continue to disproportionately harm immigrant and oppressed communities. Because ICE is a federal agency, accountability for this agency has to be a national effort with clear targets.

At the state level, in 2021, the North Carolina State Legislature passed Senate Bill 300, the Criminal Justice Reform Bill. The governor signed this into law while applauding it for aligning with many of the recommendations that came out of his Governor's Task Force for Racial Equity in Criminal Justice (TREC). Unfortunately none of the 125 recommendations focused solely on immigration enforcement, and immigrants were not represented on the task force. And while some of those TREC representatives applaud Senate Bill 300, publicly available criminal-legal data was taken out of the bill, making it challenging for the general public to have access to readily available information about the criminal-legal system. Furthermore, immigration status in this arena is challenging to come by—inquirers are often routed to federal agencies to complete data requests, or accountability is pushed back to the local instead of a statewide solution.

The North Carolina case also highlights the complicated nature of "welcoming" initiatives at the local level when you live in a state that forces multilevel and multijurisdictional policies. Without an expanded understanding of the deportation continuum (Kalir and Wissink 2016), the role of crimmigration entities (Garcia Hernandez 2015), and sealed-off political realms, we miss other potential social movement campaign targets and areas of study. Furthermore, two "unintended" results may occur: first, the further criminalization of both immigrants and nonimmigrants under probation and parole supervision, which further contributes to the narrative of "deserving" and "undeserving" immigrants, and second, the circumvention by state-level agencies and ICE of these politics and agreements even in locations where ICE no longer has an agreement with local law enforcement, raising more questions of transparency and accountability (Shepherd 2018).[1]

Every four years, local sheriff elections also draw some level of local scrutiny. This year, I helped run a series of teach-ins called "Know Your Sheriffs" with the North Carolina Statewide Police Accountability Network. Our goals were twofold: (1) to educate leaders about the role of the sheriff and (2) to make the connection between police who patrol our communities and the jails that incarcerate them. Two years ago, we also created a "Defund Sheriff" toolkit—aligned with the "Divest/Invest" framework—to make the latter point even clearer. The hope is that this approach to connect the responsibilities of various law enforcement agencies pushes us to consider those touch points and to further illustrate the reach of the carceral state.

While immigrant rights activists have mostly focused on sheriffs, and Black Lives Matter activists tend to focus on local police, there are unfortunate incidents that push these two foci together. In January 2021, our North Carolina communities experienced five police killings, possibly more, that bring the issues of accountability to the forefront of our minds. North Carolina was last to raise the age for juveniles being held in adult facilities and a pioneer in adopting 287(g) programs, but I'm hopeful that we can become a pioneer in community-based safety strategies that don't rely on law enforcement. In one of the five police killings, a Latinx immigrant man—Daniel Turcios—was shot by police in front of his wife and kids after experiencing a car accident. And the community response is a collective one—unifying Black and brown communities who see this as an injustice.

My hope is that we are building a movement invested in uncovering how we got here in the first place. We must step out of this collective amnesia and see the connections right in front of us. ICE entanglement is just one iteration of a bigger system meant to police our communities. But we can continue untangling this collaboration while we contribute to movements whose members are fed up with the criminal-legal system more broadly. And we can start in our own communities. Going back to my hometown in 2015 to conduct interviews brought me hope and made me see the possibilities for change. I hope that my family can one day live without the fear of an ICE arrest, and I know that's possible through the efforts of a thriving group of community organizers. And like many immigrant rights activists before me have said, the only secure community is an organized community.

INTRODUCTION

1. As I wrapped up field research, this would become more apparent as ICE spokespersons continued to identify the need for two of the programs to exist during heated sheriff elections in Wake and Mecklenburg Counties. While the programs in those two counties ended in the fall of 2018 after the incumbents lost their respective races, two new programs—one 287(g) program popped up in an adjacent county to Wake, and a new Intergovernmental Service Agreement (IGSA) popped up in Alamance County—may be utilized as replacement opportunities to funnel immigrants into immigrant detention, creating some additional jurisdictional navigation. The title of this chapter is the name of a song written by La Santa Cecilia, a group that "exemplifies the modern-day creative hybrid of Latin culture, rock and world music" according to their website.

2. César Cuauhtémoc García Hernández considers various local entities as crimmigration law entities, including some local law enforcement, legal counsel, etc.

CHAPTER 1

1. In Gaston County, the resolution was titled "To Adopt Policies and Apply Staff Direction Relating to Illegal Residents in Gaston County." In Mecklenburg County, the city council committee was called the Mayor's Immigration Study Commission. In Henderson County, the committee was called the Blue Ribbon Committee on Illegal Immigration.

2. Since the inception of the 287(g) program in Henderson County, 1,057 detainers have been sent for undocumented persons, and ICE assumed custody for 749 of those people. Peaks occurred in 2009 (183), 2011 (287), and 2012 (154). See http://trac.syr.edu/phptools/immigration/detain/.

3. U and T visas are reserved for undocumented individuals who have been the victims of crimes and who assist law enforcement in criminal investigations (Eagly 2010).

CHAPTER 2

1. In February 2019, ICE arrested and detained approximately 200 people across North Carolina, beginning with workplace arrests in Sanford, North Carolina, at Bear Creek Arsenal, in a coordinated effort between Homeland Security Investigations (HSI) and Lee County sheriff Tracy Lynn Carter (Terry, Magnus, and Stasio 2019).

2. Executive Order: Border Security and Immigration Enforcement Improvements is available at https://trumpwhitehouse.archives.gov/presidential-actions/executive-order-border-security-immigration-enforcement-improvements; Executive Order: Enhancing Public Safety in the Interior of the United States is available at https://trump whitehouse.archives.gov/presidential-actions/executive-order-enhancing-public-safety-interior-united-states.

3. According to FaithAction International House (2019),

> The Faith Action ID card provides card holders with a reliable form of identification that can be used as a tool by law enforcement, city departments, health centers, schools, businesses, and cultural arts organizations to better identify, serve, and protect immigrants. All participants must attend an ID drive, in which they are required to go through an orientation on the benefits and limitations of the card, and sign a simple MOU [memorandum of understanding] to this effect. They then go through a thorough vetting process in which they must provide proof of identity (embassy ID, national ID card, passport, or driver's license) and proof of address (utility bill, medical record, bank statement, or lease agreement). The required list of approved documents must be agreed upon by local law enforcement partners, and all those at the document check station must be trained and reliable. An immigration attorney or paralegal is present at each document check table as questions of authenticity arise. As one of the hallmarks of the program, participants also engage in dialogue with law enforcement and other community partners present throughout the waiting process on a variety of topics, including: how to report a crime, traffic and domestic violence laws, and navigating city, health, and social service systems. (FaithAction International House 2019)

4. While not explicitly detailed in Wacquant's 2009 *Punishing the Poor: The Neoliberal Government of Social Insecurity*, Wacquant (2010) also uses the language of "institutional tentacles" to describe the various ways control and communication are weaved together to reshape the sociosymbolic landscape and remake the state itself, citing probation, parole, criminal databases, swirling discourses about crime, and a virulent culture of public denigration of offenders as specific tentacles.

5. This is aside from individuals receiving Deferred Action for Childhood Arrivals (DACA), which was not relevant until 2012, and even this was subject to a state-by-state patchwork of allowing individuals to obtain a driver's license.

6. House Bill 318 passed in the fall of 2015, along with previously proposed legislation such as Senate Bill 145 and House Bill 113.

7. From reply to a public records request received in August 2016, the steps utilized when determining the immigration status of an arrestee at the Durham County Detention Facility:

1) An arrestee is processed and fingerprinted.
2) Fingerprints are sent electronically to the State Bureau of Investigation (SBI).

3) If the arrestee is wanted by ICE, their fingerprint is flagged through the fingerprint machine or the Finger Print Tech fills out a Notification of Arrest form and faxes it to ICE.

4) The Fingerprint Tech will print the flagged information and fax it to ICE. If needed, Immigration authorities will determine their status and issue a detainer.

5) An arrestee is allowed to leave the facility (on bond or per magistrate or judge's order) as long as a detainer has not been received.

6) If a detainer is received the detainee will remain in custody until his case is adjudicated.

7) Once all charges (for any county, or state) have been adjudicated, ICE is notified (by the arresting agency). There's a 48-hour deadline including holidays and weekends for ICE to take custody of the arrestee.

8) If ICE does not arrive within 48 hours, the detainee is released.

8. In 2008, according to the Bureau of Justice Assistance State Criminal Alien Assistance program (SCAAP), the method for determining the payment formula was as follows:

a. Using financial data from applicants, a per diem rate is calculated for each jurisdiction. For FY2007, the average per diem rate was $30.30 per inmate.

b. Inmate data is provided to the U.S. Department of Homeland Security to validate inmate data for eligible, unknown, and invalid records.

c. Each jurisdiction's total eligible inmate days and a percentage of the unknown days are totaled then multiplied by the applicant's per diem rate to derive the total correctional officer salary costs for eligible and unknown inmate days. The percentage used for unknown days is determined by a sliding scale: citizens 60 percent, states 65 percent, and counties 80 percent of their total unknown inmate days.

d. The value of each applicant's correctional officer salary costs associated with its eligible and credited unknown inmate days are totaled. This total value reflects the maximum amount for SCAAP reimbursement. A percentage factor is used to reflect the relationship between the maximum reimbursable salary costs and the appropriation. For FY2007, this factor was approximately 41.98 percent.

More information is available at https://bja.ojp.gov/program/state-criminal-alien -assistance-program-scaap/archives.

CHAPTER 3

1. Robbins, Simonsen, and Feldman (2008) describe this phenomenon as it pertains to web-based citizen participation in administrative decision-making processes. Drawing on public choice theory to explain citizen involvement in government decisions, they highlight instances when it is rational to not spend time on

a particular issue if the gain does not outweigh the time spent becoming educated about it. They go on to say, "In particular, this is true for government services that are collectively paid for and consumed—because citizens ae unaware of the link between the benefits they receive and the amount they pay. . . . The majority of citizens do not appear to have concerns intense enough to provoke participation and information gathering. Citizens are generally satisfied with their public services" (564). As Justice and Dülger describe it, "rational ignorance can result from scarcity of analytic skills as well as time, from information overload, and from poor communication or presentation by suppliers of information," whereas irrational ignorance results from "the lack of a general culture of information use or an aversion to using financial information in particular" (2009, 267)

2. "We recently approved the U-visa. U-visa enables temporary citizenship even to an illegal alien. We approve U-visas in this particular case because it was for a female and her daughter had been sexually molested by her father. We need the testimony of that illegal alien in order to convict that person that was sexually molesting that small child, so we granted a U-visa, and I signed that paper" (May 3, 2010, Henderson County Board of Commissioners meeting).

3. These two goals were described at the September 4, 2012, Henderson County Board of Commissioners meeting:

Goal #7: Support NC drivers permit for agricultural workers. Goal description: support legislation making it possible for individuals actively working in agriculture to get a NC permit allowing them to drive without regards to their citizenship, thereby insuring an adequate workforce for farm operations, a means for workers to legally travel to and from work and other locations as needed, and enable better enforcement of proper motor vehicle insurance, as well as insuring proper training of operators, who will be on the road regardless. *All voted in favor and the motion carried.*

Goal #8: Support suspension of mandatory use of E-verify (NC HB36) for agriculture. Goal Description: Suspend the requirement for employers in the agricultural sector, under HB36, to participate in the federal E-verification program until the Federal Government has addressed the issue of a Guest Worker Visa system that allows for an adequate and legal workforce for agriculture, whereby the suspense of the state level requirement would protect our number one industry which is highly dependent upon immigrant labor and without which, the result would be devastating to this vital part of our economy. *Motion to send, passed 3–2 with Commissioner O'Connor and Young voting nay.* (Henderson County BOC 2012, 19)

4. As I often do, I left my recorder running at my seat when I got up to speak with a few community members in the room. In line with the comments made about making communities safer, one of the ICE officials commented, "My advice to you, don't commit a crime. If you know someone that has committed a crime, don't associate

with them." This statement completely disregards any acknowledgment that being arrested for a crime is not the same thing as committing a crime and the spillover effects of contact with the criminal-legal system.

5. Included in this resolution was the following:

Cease and desist local funding for any local programs provided to non-qualified illegal residents. Discontinue all federally funded non-mandated programs servicing illegal residents. Discontinue all state funded non-mandated programs servicing illegal residents. Discontinue contracting with any local or out-of-county businesses employing or using identifiable illegal residents where county tax dollars are being expended. Update minimum housing requirements to address the number of individuals/families that can be accommodated in rental dwellings. County funded law enforcement agencies and the County Sheriff are instructed to diligently battle the ever-increasing criminal element which is growing daily with the influx of the illegal population and to consistently check the immigration status of each undocumented resident upon his/her arrest by means consisting of but not limited to accessible data, finger prints, and/or federally verified social security numbers rather than tax identification numbers. Allow County Police to partner with ICE to verify undocumented residents during any minor/major public safety infraction and if identified as undocumented, detain for deportation. Without the ability to legally discern citizenship and based only on estimates of County services, any and all county health departments or agencies are instructed to begin expenditure reductions for discretionary services provided to illegal aliens. (Gaston County BOC 2006b, 17)

6. In 2013, the county manager ran an online survey between May 28 and June 11 where over 4,000 individuals responded to questions about the county budget. All respondents resided, worked, or owned a business in Gaston County. Of the respondents 59.4 percent were between the ages of thirty-five and fifty-four, 86 percent were homeowners, 72 percent owned a home valued between $100,000 and $300,000, and the cities of Belmont and Cherryville were overrepresented (Gaston County BOC 2013). The seven questions asked were:

1) Do you live or work in Gaston County?
2) How important is it to you that Gaston has the following resources?
   [A number of choices were provided with a scoring of 1–5.]
3) How much funding should the County give to Gaston County Schools next year?
4) What operating funding level should the County Provide to Gaston College next year?
5) Public Safety[?]
6) Community Services[?]
7) Human Services[?]

7. Wildin was just one of the NC6—high school–aged migrants who would be detained by ICE (Bouloubasis 2017).

8. See chapter 6 for more information on the various types of partnerships; I explicitly asked whether Sheriff Miller had considered his office's response were Homeland Security Investigations (HSI)—the agency that collaborated with the Sanford, North Carolina, Sheriff's Office to arrest workers at a gun-manufacturing plant in early 2019—to request his collaboration. In that exchange, he responded that he needed to look into the matter further.

CHAPTER 4

1. This statement came from the first interview I conducted in Henderson County in 2015.

2. An immigrant's ability to apply for a U-Visa after being the victim of particular crimes was often cited as the exemplary outcome of cooperation between local law enforcement and the Latinx immigrant community—because a mandatory requirement of the U-Visa application is a signed certificate by a law enforcement agency indicating that the victim was helping in the investigation or prosecution—yet, in Durham County, approval ratings were low (UNC School of Law Immigration/Human Rights Policy Clinic and ASISTA 2019). In Orange County, approval ratings were increased by a change in the policy, and the Orange County Sheriff's Office stopped the use of detainers in their detention facility so when they state, "we are not ICE," they are actually making a substantively different claim. Elsewhere, those in the UNC School of Law Immigration/Human Rights Policy Clinic and ASISTA found that

> the U visa holds out promise to those who have suffered as crime victims and at the same time, promotes improved community relations with law enforcement and other investigatory agencies. Despite the salutary purposes of the statute, immigrant and civil rights advocates have observed that there is no uniformity among U visa certification processes, as the decision whether to sign a U visa certification is within discretion of that law enforcement agency. For this reason, certification practices vary among different law enforcement agencies and in different jurisdictions. As a result, some immigrant victims who meet the statutory elements are successful in obtaining the signed I-918B certification form and, ultimately, the U visa. Other immigrant victims with virtually identical fact patterns are often denied certification by agencies whose policies run contrary to the Congressional intent in establishing the U visa program. These applicants, thus, have no chance to obtain consideration of their U visa application by USCIS as they are unable to meet the requirement of submitting an I-918B certification. (2)

3. At the time, Mecklenburg County was the only county that would upload recent statistics about the number and country of origin of those identified immigrants.

4. There was a cooling-off period for activists immediately after the first few years

of implementation, but there has always been a small group of people who have continued to hold vigils, rallies, and the like across the state.

5. Deputy McDonald made this statement at the April 12, 2017, LINK meeting to distance the current sheriff administration from the previous sheriff.

CHAPTER 5

1. Other publicly available data conflicts with this information presented by ICE officials. According to TRAC, for the same time periods the following numbers are provided for 2016 and 2017, although whether or not ICE assumed custody after a detainer was sent is no longer being provided by ICE: for the Wake County Sheriff Department, in 2016, 379 (detainers sent), in 2017, 744 (detainers sent); for the Mecklenburg County Detention Center North, in 2016, 42 (detainers sent), in 2017, 175 (detainers sent); and for Mecklenburg County Jail Central, in 2016, 256 (detainers sent), in 2017, 403 (detainers sent). Additional data concerning SCAAP awards also suggests conflicting information: for Wake County, in 2016, 225, in 2017, 244; and for Mecklenburg County, in 2016, 386, in 2017, 228.

2. This information is taken from informational materials co-constructed between the author and the cofounders of Comunidad Colectiva as a volunteer service. They are available upon request and will be publicly available once a much larger collection of public records requests is thoroughly analyzed.

3. These were the questions for sheriff and county commissioner candidates, respectively:

What experience qualifies you to serve as sheriff? What is the most pressing issue you would pursue if elected? If elected, what would be your car chase policy? How should the department participate in tackling the growing opioid epidemic? How should the jails handle transgender individuals considering state and federal laws have not adapted to include their needs? What have you identified as training priorities and how do you plan to address them? How will you recruit and retain enough qualified people to fully staff the department? How will you handle changes to the county jails as the state moves the juvenile court age from 16–18 in Dec. 2019?

What is your stance on collaboration with federal immigration enforcement? What are some steps you would take to keep incarcerated individuals safe and connected to family members and the community? What do you believe is the appropriate level of collaboration between federal Immigration and Customs Enforcement and the _____ Office? Should NC cities and counties have the ability to establish community/civilian oversight boards with subpoena power? What policies do you support to help minimize racial bias in stops and searchers (ex: using data to flag high-disparity officer)?

4. This coalition changed its name to Familias SI, Migra NO (loosely translated as Families Yes, ICE No), indicating a change from solely challenging the 287(g)

program to recognizing that ICE cooperation, collaboration, and the like extends beyond that program.

5. Questions on the scorecard (see fig. 5.4) were constructed by a coalition of local partners and ACLU-National based on issues relevant to all parties. Questions included:

Wants to end the county's partnership with ICE, which the Trump Administration is using to deport hundreds of Mecklenburg residents.
Wants to end the use of solitary confinement for juveniles in county jails, a
practice the NAACP has described as "torture."
Wants to allow external, independent investigation of misconduct or criminal behavior in the Sheriff's Office, such as if a person is killed by law
enforcement.
Wants to restore in-person visitation between incarcerated people and their
family which helps with reintegration upon release.

6. The People's Alliance endorsed Mike Andrews in 2014, providing the following context: "The People's Alliance PAC endorses Mike Andrews for a full term as Durham County Sheriff. Andrews is from Durham and has risen through the ranks at the sheriff's office. He was picked by Sheriff Hill as his successor and was appointed by the BOCC to fill Sheriff Hill's unexpired term beginning in 2012. Mike is a fine law enforcement official with a solid record of law enforcement management. We like that he is a part of, and has continued, a culture of policing that is personal, personable, and moderate. Andrews is always accessible and responsive. In his tenure he has ad-dressed long festering complaints about the unsanitary conditions at the jail. We like that he places emphasis in updating communications and technology systems at the sheriff's office. We look to Andrews to encourage advancement within the ranks of the department for deputies and employees from every background" (www.durhampa. org/fall_2014_endorsements).

7. For example, Camilo Coronilla's—wife and daughters came to the press con-ference on behalf of Camilo Coronilla, who was arrested and subject to deportation around the time the Baker was elected. Baker wanted to end this kind of deportation pipeline but wouldn't officially enter office for a few more weeks. (Tauss 2018).

8. Of the sheriffs with 287(g) programs in North Carolina at the beginning of 2018, the Mecklenburg County sheriff was a registered Democrat. A neighboring sheriff, Sheriff Clonginer in Gaston County, is also a registered Democrat and has received awards for cooperation with ICE.

## CONCLUSION

1. Multnomah County, Oregon, sheriff Mike Reese doesn't allow his office to pro-vide mug shots or booking reports to ICE. As a result, the U.S. Marshal Service shares it with ICE: "The Marshals Service, which rents beds in Multnomah County jails, regularly sends lists created by Reese's office containing names of federal inmates

held in Portland jails to ICE—without informing the Sheriff. . . . The Marshals Service confirms it's sharing the reports. 'We share information on a regular, routine basis with the federal partners that have a need to know where the inmates in our federal custody are houses,' says Pete Cajigal, deputy chief of the U.S. Marshals Service, Oregon District. 'We send it to ICE on a regular basis'" (Shepherd 2018).

Achenbaum, Emily, S. 2007a. "Screening of Inmates' Citizenship Proposed." *Raleigh News and Observer*, September 1. http://docs.newsbank.com/s/InfoWeb /aggdocs/AWNB/11B64F2827F2C2C8/0D0CB4F32A21A855?p_multi=RLOB&s_lang =en-US. Accessed August 19, 2014. No longer available online.

———. 2007b. "Prisons Chief Says No Thanks, Myrick." *Raleigh News and Observer*, September 11. http://docs.newsbank.com/s/InfoWeb/aggdocs/AWNB/11B99B98 E03B0D88/0D0CB4F32A21A855?p_multi=RLOB&s_lang=en-US. Accessed August 19, 2014. No longer available online.

Alsous, Zaina. 2019. "'Starve the Beast': Southern Campaigns to Divest, Decarcerate, and Re-imagine public safety." Racial Justice Action Center, November 4. www.rjactioncenter.org/post/media-starve-the-beast-southern-campaigns-to -divest-decarcerate-and-re-imagine-public-safety.

American Immigration Council. 2012. "The 287(g) Program: A Flawed and Obsolete Method of Immigration Enforcement." November. www.americanimmigration council.org/sites/default/files/research/287g_fact_sheet_11–2012_0.pdf.

Aranda, E., C. Menjívar, and K. M. Donato. 2014. "The Spillover Consequences of an Enforcement-First U.S. Immigration Regime." *American Behavioral Scientist* 58 (November): 1687–95.

Armenta, Amada. 2012. "From Sheriff's Deputies to Immigration Officers: Screening Immigrant Status in a Tennessee Jail." *Law and Policy* 34 (January): 191–210.

———. 2015. "Between Public Service and Social Control: Policing Dilemmas in the Era of Immigration Enforcement." *Social Problems* 63 (February): 111–26.

Arriaga, Felicia. 2017. "Relationships between the Public and Crimmigration Entities in North Carolina: A 287(g) Program Focus." *Sociology of Race and Ethnicity* 3 (July): 417–31.

Barber, Rebekah. 2018. "Voices of Resistance: How to Unseat an ICE-Collaborating Sheriff." Facing South. www.facingsouth.org/2018/11/voices-resistance-how -unseat-ice-collaborating-sheriff.

Beach, D., and R. Pedersen. 2013. *Process-Tracing Methods: Foundations and Guidelines*. Ann Arbor: University of Michigan Press.

Bell, Adam. 2017. "Meck Sheriff to Community: We Don't Decide Who Gets Deported by ICE." *Charlotte Observer*, March 2. www.charlotteobserver.com/news /local/article135984403.html. No longer available online.

Bellamy, Cliff. 2018. "Judge Orders Wildin Acosta Deported, but Not Yet. Here's Why." *Raleigh News and Observer*, January 3. www.newsobserver.com/news/local /counties/durham-county/article192782069.html.

Berman, G., and Y. Paradies. 2010. "Racism, Disadvantage and Multiculturalism:

Towards Effective Anti-racist Praxis." *Ethnic and Racial Studies* 33 (August): 214–32.

Bernal, D. D. 1998. "Using a Chicana Feminist Epistemology in Educational Research." *Harvard Education Review* 68, no. 4 (January): 555–58.

Bex, S., and S. Craps. 2016. "Humanitarianism, Testimony, and the White Savior Industrial Complex: What Is the What versus Kony 2012." *Cultural Critique*, January, 32–56.

Billman, Jeffrey. 2019. "ICE, a Perfectly Normal Government Agency, Creates Website to Shame and Threaten North Carolina Sheriffs." *IndyWeek*, November 21. www.indyweek.com/news/northcarolina/ice-website-north-carolina-sheriffs/.

Birkhead, Clarence. 2019. "Community Advisory Board." Durham Sheriff YouTube channel. www.youtube.com/watch?v=kokj8dVAPLc.

BJA (Bureau of Justice Assistance). n.d. "State Criminal Alien Assistance Program (SCAAP) Award Guide." https://bja.ojp.gov/program/state-criminal-alien -assistance-program-scaap/archives. Accessed October 12, 2022.

———. 2012. "State Criminal Alien Assistance Program (SCAAP): Overview." March 4. https://bja.ojp.gov/program/state-criminal-alien-assistance-program -scaap/overview. Updated April 22, 2021.

Blalock, Hubert. 1967. *Toward a Theory of Minority Group Relations*. New York: Wiley and Sons.

Blue, Victor. 2017. "North Carolina Immigrant ID Card Praised by Police Is in Jeopardy." NBC News, June 7. www.nbcnews.com/news/latino/north-carolina -immigrant-id-card-praised-police-jeopardy-n764106.

Blumer, Herbert. 1958. "Race Prejudice as a Sense of Group Position." *Pacific Sociological Review* 1 (March): 3–7.

Blythe, Anne. 2018. "ICE Picks Up Durham Man Days before Hearing on Legality of 48 Hour Hold." *Raleigh News and Observer*, May 27. www.newsobserver.com /news/local/article211996234.html.

Bolter, Jessica, Emma Israel, and Sarah Pierce. 2022. "Four Years of Profound Change: Immigration Policy during the Trump Presidency." Migration Policy Institute, February. www.migrationpolicy.org/research/four-years-change -immigration-trump.

Bonilla-Silva, Eduardo. 2014. *Racism without Racists: Color-Blind Racism and the Persistence of Racial Inequality in the United States*. Lanham, Md.: Rowman and Littlefield.

Bouloubasis, Victoria. 2017. "Wildin Acosta's Detention Sparked a Community into Action, but He's Still Not Free." *IndyWeek*, March 22. https://indyweek.com /guides/archives/wildin-acosta-s-detention-sparked-community-action-still-free/.

Bridges, George S., Robert D. Crutchfeld, and Edith E. Simpson. 1987. "Crime, Social Structure and Criminal Punishment: White and Nonwhite Rates of Imprisonment." *Social Problems* 34 (October): 345–61. http://heinonlinebackup .com/hol-cgi-bin/get_pdf.cgi?handle=hein.journals/socprob34&section=32.

Bridges, Virginia, and Mark Schults. 2015. "Durham Police Chief Jose Lopez to Retire at Year's End." *Raleigh News and Observer*, September 15. www.newsobserver .com/news/local/counties/durham-county/article35315001.html.

Bronstein, Phoebe. 2015. "Comic Relief: The Andy Griffith Show, White Southern Sheriffs, and Regional Rehabilitation." *Camera Obscura* 30, no. 89 (September): 125–55.

Brown, Craig M., and Barbara D. Warner. 1992. "Immigrants, Urban Politics, and Policing in 1900." *American Sociological Review* 57 (June): 293–305.

Brown, J. 2017. "Outrage, Fear as ICE Cracks Down in Immigration Raids." ABC 11, February 15. http://abc11.com/politics/outrage-fear-as-ice-cracks-down-in-immigration-raids/1753441/.

Building Integrated Communities. 2022. Latino Migration Project. https://migration.unc.edu/building-integrated-communities/. Accessed June 20, 2022.

Cabarrus County Board of Commissioners. 2007. Budget Report. https://docs.cabarruscounty.us/WebLink/DocView.aspx?id=1879544&page=156&searchid=bd637874-0135-4dde-8d50-72f64f551e9b.

———. 2010. Budget Report. https://docs.cabarruscounty.us/WebLink/ElectronicFile.aspx?docid=1879540&dbid=1. 2010 Budget Report.

———. 2014. Budget Report. https://docs.cabarruscounty.us/WebLink/ElectronicFile.aspx?docid=1736662&dbid=1 . 2014 Budget Report.

———. 2018. Budget Report. https://docs.cabarruscounty.us/WebLink/ElectronicFile.aspx?docid=1616966&dbid=1 . 2018 Budget Report.

Calderon, S. M. 2012. "The Extent of Political Participation in the United States among Latino Non-citizens and Citizens." *McNair Scholars Research Journal* 5, no. 1: 19–32. https://commons.emich.edu/mcnair/vol5/iss1/4/.

Capital Tonight Staff. 2019. "Rep. Destin Hall on ICE Cooperation Bill." *Spectrum News*, March 21. https://spectrumlocalnews.com/nc/charlotte/capital-tonight-interviews/2019/03/21/rep—destin-hall-on-ice-cooperation-bill.

*Charlotte Observer*. 2006. "Mecklenburg Holds Illegal Immigrants." November 29. http://docs.newsbank.com/s/InfoWeb/aggdocs/AWNB/115B5AAEA3FC5378/0D0CB4F32A21A855?p_multi=RLOB&s_lang=en-US. Accessed August 19, 2014. No longer available online.

Chavez, Jorge M., and Doris M. Provine. 2009. "Race and the Response of State Legislatures to Unauthorized Immigrants." *Annals of the American Academy* 623 (May): 78–92.

Chavez, Leo R. 2013. *The Latino Threat: Constructing Immigrants, Citizens, and the Nation*. Stanford, Calif.: Stanford University Press.

Chen, Pamela K. 2015. "Innovation at the Front Lines." *New York Law School Law Review* 60 (January): 623–30.

Chicurel-Bayard, Dustin. 2014. "Community Supports Durham FADE Recommendations." Southern Coalition for Social Justice. www.southerncoalition.org/community-shows-support-durham-fade-recommendations-2/. Accessed September 15, 2018.

Cole, T. 2012. "The White-Savior Industrial Complex." *Atlantic*, March 21. www.theatlantic.com/international/archive/2012/03/the-white-savior-industrial-complex/254843/.

Coleman, Mathew. 2009. "What Counts as the Politics and Practice of Security, and Where? Devolution and Immigrant Insecurity after 9/11." *Annals of the Association of American Geographers* 99 (November): 904–13.

———. 2012. "The 'Local' Migration State: The Site-Specific Devolution of Immigration Enforcement in the U.S. South." *Law and Policy* 34 (April): 159–90.

Collins, Kristin. 2007. "N.C. Leads in Immigrant Crackdown." *Raleigh News and Observer*, October 18. http://docs.newsbank.com/s/InfoWeb/aggdocs/AWNB /11C5CCB5503673A0/0D0CB4F32A21A855?p_multi=RLOB&s_lang=en-US. Accessed August 18, 2014. No longer available online.

———. 2008. "Children Ended Up Alone for Hours." *Charlotte Observer*, July 23. www.charlotteobserver.com/news/local/article8994665.html.

Comunidad Colectiva. 2020. https://comunidadcolectiva.org/about/.

Covington, Owen. 2018. "ELON POLL: N.C. Voters More Tuned in to Leaders in Washington Than to Those Governing In Raleigh." Elon.edu, February 23. www .elon.edu/u/news/2018/02/23/elon-poll-%E2%80%8Bn-c-voters-more-tuned-in-to -leaders-in-washington-than-to-those-governing-in-raleigh/.

Critical Resistance. 2020a. "Reformist Reforms vs. Abolitionist Steps in Policing." https://criticalresistance.org/resources/reformist-reforms-vs-abolitionist-steps -in-policing/.

———. 2020b. "Abolitionist Steps to End Imprisonment—New Organizing Resource." https://criticalresistance.org/updates/abolitionist-steps-to-end -imprisonment-new-organizing-resource/.

DeGrave, Sam. 2018. "ICE Challenged at Public Meeting over 287(g), No Supporters Speak Out among Crowd of 40." *Citizen Times*, April 25. www.citizen-times.com /story/news/local/2018/04/25/ice-challenged-public-meeting-over-287-g-no -supporters-speak-out-among-crowd-40/545741002/.

Delgado, R., and J. Stefancic. 2000. *Critical Race Theory: The Cutting Edge*. Philadelphia: Temple University Press.

Denning Riggsbee, Shea. 2009. "The Impact of North Carolina Driver's License Requirements and the REAL ID Act of 2005 on Unauthorized Immigrants." *Popular Government* 74 (April): 1–14.

Detention Watch Network. 2022. "Ending Immigrant Detention: Abolitionist Steps vs. Reformist Reforms." www.detentionwatchnetwork.org/freethemall. Accessed October 24, 2022.

Doty, Roxanne Lynne, and Elizabeth Shannon Wheatley. 2013. "Private Detention and the Immigration Industrial Complex." *International Political Sociology* 7 (December): 426–43. doi:10.1111/ips.12032.

Durham Human Relations Commission. 2017. "Recommendations: Durham County Detention Facility." January 3. https://www.durhamnc.gov/Document Center/View/20151/Durham-County-Detention-Facility-Recommendations.

Durkee, Alison. 2017. "Federal Immigration Agent Looking for Fourth-Grader at NYC School Blocked from Entering." Mic, May 14. https://mic.com/articles /177108/ice-agents-looking-for-4th-grade-student-at-nyc-school-blocked-from -entering#.lk7iT8xC6.

Eagly, Ingrid V. 2010. "Prosecuting Immigration." *Northwestern University Law Review* 104 (August): 1281–360.

Elon Poll. 2018. "The State of Political Knowledge in North Carolina." www.elon .edu/e/CmsFile/GetFile?FileID=1234.

FaithAction International House. 2017. "FaithAction ID Impact Document." https://faithaction.org/wp-content/uploads/2019/07/2019-FaithAction-ID-Program-and-Network-Overview.pdf. Accessed October 24, 2022.

———. 2019. "FaithAction ID Program." https://faithaction.org/faithaction-id-program-and-network. Accessed October 12, 2022.

Familias SI, 287(g) NO. 2018. "The Wake County Sheriff Election." Facebook, October 29. www.facebook.com/events/257313824983028/?active_tab=about.

Farris, Emily M., and Mirya R. Holman. 2017. "All Politics Is Local? County Sheriffs and Localized Policies of Immigration Enforcement." *Political Research Quarterly* 70 (March): 142–54.

Feldblum, Sam. 2018. "ICE Raids Shine Spotlight on Henderson County's 287(g) Program." *Mountain Express*, May 3. https://mountainx.com/news/ice-raids-shine-spotlight-on-henderson-countys-287g-program/.

Fisher Williamson, Abigail. 2018. *Welcoming New Americans? Local Governments and Immigrant Incorporation.* Chicago: University of Chicago Press.

Flaherty, J. 2016. *No More Heroes: Grassroots Challenges to the Savior Mentality.* AK Press.

Fragomen, A. T. 1997. "The Illegal Immigration Reform and Immigrant Responsibility Act of 1996: An Overview." *International Migration Review* 31 (June): 438–60.

Fussell, Elizabeth. 2014. "Warmth of the Welcome: Attitudes Toward Immigrants and Immigration Policy in the United States." *Annual Review of Sociology* 40 (January): 479–98. doi:10.1146/annurev-soc-071913-043325.

Gallagher, Charles A., and Cameron D. Lippard. 2011. *Being Brown in Dixie: Race, Ethnicity, and Latino Immigration in the New South.* Latinos: Exploring Diversity and Change. Boulder, Colo.: Lynne Rienner.

GAO (U.S. Government Accountability Office). 2009. "Immigration Enforcement: Better Controls Needed over Program Authorizing State and Local Enforcement of Federal Immigration Laws," January 30. www.gao.gov/products/gao-09-109.

García Hernández, César Cuauhtémoc. 2014. "Creating Crimmigration." *Brigham Young University Law Review* 6 (February): 1457–516.

———. 2015. *Crimmigration Law.* American Bar Association.

Gaston County BOC (Board of Commissioners). 2006a. Meeting Minutes, May 11. https://egov.gastongov.com/WebLink/DocView.aspx?id=1272699&dbid=0&repo=GCLF.

———. 2006b. Meeting Minutes, November 9. https://egov.gastongov.com/WebLink/DocView.aspx?id=1272712&dbid=0&repo=GCLF.

———. 2006c. Meeting Minutes, December 14. https://egov.gastongov.com/WebLink/DocView.aspx?id=1272714&dbid=0&repo=GCLF.

———. 2008. Meeting Minutes, February 28. https://egov.gastongov.com/WebLink/DocView.aspx?id=1272740&dbid=0&repo=GCLF.

———. 2013. Meeting Minutes, June 13. https://egov.gastongov.com/WebLink/DocView.aspx?id=2075305&dbid=0&repo=GCLF.

———. 2013–14. Budget Report. In author's possession.

George, Alexander, and Andrew Bennett. 2005. *Case Studies and Theory Development in the Social Sciences*. BCSIA Studies in International Security. Cambridge, Mass.: MIT Press.

Golash-Boza, Tanya, and Pierette Hondagneu-Sotelo. 2013. "Latino Immigrant Men and the Deportation Crisis: A Gendered Racial Removal Program." *Latino Studies* 11 (September): 271–92.

Gonzales, Richard. 2019. "No ICE Arrests in Courthouses without Judicial Warrants, N.Y. Court Directive Says." NPR, April 18. www.npr.org/2019/04/17/714496186/new-york-courts-tell-ice-not-to-arrest-immigrants-in-courthouses-without-warrant.

"Guest Contributor." 2020. "Immigrant Rights Group RAICES Action Releases Candidate Scorecard Ahead of Super Tuesday." Latino Rebels, March 3. https://www.latinorebels.com/2020/03/03/raicescandidatescorecard.

Gulasekaram, Pratheepan, and S. Karthick Ramakrishnan. 2015. *The New Immigration Federalism*. Cambridge: Cambridge University Press.

Green, Jordan. 2017. "Limited Cooperation with ICE by Sheriff Seen as Tough on Immigration." *Triad City Beat*, May 31. https://triad-city-beat.com/limited-cooperation-ice-sheriff-seen-tough-immigration/.

Green, Miranda. 2017. "New Bill Aims to Block ICE from Identifying as Police Officers." CNN, April 6. www.cnn.com/2017/04/06/politics/ice-officers-police-bill/index.html.

Harbin, John. 2010. "Immigration Law's Opponents, Backers Speak Up." BlueRidgeNow.com, May 4. www.blueridgenow.com/article/NC/20100504/News/606017067/HT.

Hellerstein, Erica. 2017. "Police Chief: No More Checkpoints in Durham." *Indyweek*, March 5. www.indyweek.com/news/archives/2017/03/05/police-chief-no-more-checkpoints-in-durham.

Henderson County BOC (Board of Commissioners). 2007a. "Blue Ribbon Committee on Illegal Immigration Final Report." August 6. www.hendersoncountync.gov/sites/default/files/archives/Meetings/Board_of_Commissioners/agenda071017/DI.A.pdf.

———. 2007b. Meeting Minutes, October 17. www.hendersoncountync.gov/sites/default/files/archives/Meetings/Board_of_Commissioners/071017m.htm.

———. 2008a. Meeting Minutes, February 20. www.hendersoncountync.gov/sites/default/files/archives/Meetings/Board_of_Commissioners/080220m.htm.

———. 2008b. Meeting Minutes, March 19. www.hendersoncountync.gov/sites/default/files/archives/Meetings/Board_of_Commissioners/080319m.htm.

———. 2008c. Meeting Minutes, August 12. www.hendersoncountync.gov/sites/default/files/archives/Meetings/Board_of_Commissioners/080812m.htm.

———. 2009. Meeting Minutes, January 21. www.hendersoncountync.gov/sites/default/files/archives/Meetings/Board_of_Commissioners/090121m.htm.

———. 2010. Meeting Minutes, August 2. www.hendersoncountync.gov/boc/page/board-commissioners-meeting-191.

———. 2012. Meeting Minutes, September 4. https://www.hendersoncountync.gov/boc/page/board-commissioners-meeting-1230.

———. 2014. Meeting Minutes, May 22. www.hendersoncountync.gov/sites/default /files/fileattachments/board_of_commissioners/meeting/113702/140522m.pdf.

Hernandez, Salvador. 2018a. "Hurricane Florence Has Left Farmworkers Stranded Without Work, Food, Or Aid." Buzzfeed News, September 28. www.buzzfeed news.com/article/salvadorhernandez/farmworkers-hurricane-florence-north -carolina.

———. 2018b. "These Migrant Workers Called 911 During Hurricane Florence. But No One Came To Their Rescue." Buzzfeed News, October 1. www.buzzfeednews .com/article/salvadorhernandez/migrant-workers-stranded-hurricane-florence.

Herrington, Cass. 2019. "Henderson Co. Still Dealing with Fallout from ICE Arrests." Blue Ridge Public Radio, April 25. www.bpr.org/post/henderson-co-still -dealing-fallout-ice-arrests.

———. 2020. "Fall Harvest Brings New Challenges During Pandemic." WFAE News, October 2. www.wfae.org/local-news/2020-10-02/fall-harvest-brings-new -challenges-during-pandemic.

Hoefer, Michael, Nancy Rytina, and Bryan C. Baker. 2011. *Estimates of the Unauthorized Immigrant Population Residing in the United States: January 2010*. Washington, D.C.: Office of Immigration Statistics, U.S. Department of Homeland Security.

Huddle, Jason. 2018. "The Midterm Elections: Meet the Candidates." *Cabarrus Magazine*, October. www.cabarrusmagazine.com/2018/10/01/180895/the-midterm -elections-meet-the-candidates.

ICE (U.S. Immigration and Customs Enforcement). 2007. ICE ACCESS (ICE Agreements of Cooperation in Communities to Enhance Safety and Security) Fact Sheet. American Immigration Lawyers Association, August 22. www.aila.org /infonet/ice-access-fact-sheet.

———. 2009. "Secure Communities Program Presentations." www.ice.gov/doclib /foia/secure_communities/securecommunitiespresentations.pdf.

ICE of out CA. 2022. http://www.iceoutofca.org/. Accessed June 20, 2022.

ILRC (Immigration Law Resource Center). 2021. "ICE Detainers: Strategies & Considerations for Criminal Defense Counsel." December 2021. www.ilrc.org/sites /default/files/resources/ice_detainers-_advice_and_strategies_for_criminal _defense_counsel.pdf.

Indy Staff. 2018. "For Durham County Sheriff, the INDY Endorses Clarence Birkhead." *Indyweek*, April 18. www.indyweek.com/indyweek/for-durham-county -sheriff-the-indy-endorses-clarence-birkhead/Content?oid=13460372.

Jacobs, David, and Ronald Helms. 1999. "Collective Outbursts, Politics, and Punitive Resources: Toward a Political Sociology of Spending on Social Control." *Social Forces* 77 (June): 1497–523.

Jaffe, Alexandra. 2021. "'Do Not Come': Harris Seeks 'Hope at Home' for Guatemalans." Associated Press, June 7. https://apnews.com/article/health-coronavirus -pandemic-immigration-business-government-and-politics-1f0ea4ef33f37d62ccd 3cf867d71d017.

Johnson, Jeh Charles. 2014. "Policies for the Apprehension, Detention and Removal of Undocumented Immigrants." U.S. Department of Homeland Security,

November 20. www.dhs.gov/sites/default/files/publications/14_1120_memo
_prosecutorial_discretion.pdf. Accessed March 20, 2015.

Justice, Jonathan, and Cumhur Dülger. 2009. "Fiscal Transparency and Authentic Citizenship Participation in Public Budgeting the Role of the Third Party Intermediation." *Journal of Budgeting, Accounting and Financial Management* 21 (March): 254–87.

Kahn, Carrie. 2021. "On Mexico's Southern Border, the Latest Migration Surge Is Haitian." NPR, December 18. www.npr.org/2021/12/18/1065135970/on-mexicos
-southern-border-the-latest-migration-surge-is-haitian.

Kalir, Barak, and Lieke Wissink. 2016. "The Deportation Continuum: Convergences between State-Agents and NGO-Workers in the Dutch Deportation Field." *Citizenship Studies* 20, no. 1:34–49.

Kandel, William. 2016. "U.S. Immigration Policy: Chart Book of Key Trends." Congressional Research Service, March 14. https://crsreports.congress.gov/product
/pdf/R/R42988/15.

Kane, Robert. 2003. "Social Control in the Metropolis: A Community-Level Examination of the Minority Group-Threat Hypothesis." *Justice Quarterly* 20 (August): 265–95.

Killian, Joe. 2018. "Black Sheriffs Make History in Sweep of Seven Largest NC Counties." NC Policy Watch, November 8. https://ncpolicywatch.com/2018/11/08
/black-sheriffs-make-history-in-sweep-of-seven-largest-nc-counties/.

Kim, Claire Jean. 1999. "The Racial Triangulation of Asian Americans." *Politics and Society* 27 (March): 105–38.

Lacey, D. 2017. "Immigration: Ag Leaders Speak Out as Employees Skip Work." BlueRidgeNow.com, February 17. www.blueridgenow.com/story/news/politics
/2017/02/17/immigration-ag-leaders-speak-out-as-employees-skip-work
/22439608007.

Lamb, Amanda. 2018. "Orange Sheriff, ICE Square Off over Release of Inmates in US Illegally." WRAL News, July 25. www.wral.com/orange-sheriff-ice-square-off
-over-release-of-inmates-in-us-illegally/17724377/.

Langarica, Monika. 2015. "'We Never Even Saw the Sunlight': How DHS Uses Deportations to Undermine Sentencing Reform." Latino Rebels, November 9. www
.latinorebels.com/2015/11/09/we-never-even-saw-the-sunlight-how-dhs-uses
-deportations-to-undermine-sentencing-reform/.

Lawson, Adam. 2017. "ICE: 64 Gaston Inmates Processed for Deportation in FY2016." *Gaston Gazette*, May 31. www.gastongazette.com/story/news/2017/05/31
/ice-64-gaston-inmates-processed-for-deportation-in-fy-2016/20753488007/.

Leal, David. 2002. "Political Participation by Latino Non-citizens in the United States." *British Journal of Political Science* 41 (April): 309–17.

Leighley, Jan, and Jonathan Nagle. 2013. *Who Votes Now? Demographics, Issues, Inequality, and Turnout in the United States.* Princeton, N.J.: Princeton University Press.

Lewis, Paul G., Doris Marie Provine, Monica W. Varsanyi, and Scott H. Decker. 2013. "Why Do (Some) City Police Departments Enforce Federal Immigration

Law? Political, Demographic, and Organizational Influences on Local Choices." *Journal of Public Administration Research and Theory* 23 (January): 1–25.

Light, Michael T. 2015. "Legal Inequality's Newest Face." *Contexts* 14 (August): 32–37.

Light, Michael, Michael Massoglia, and Ryan D. King. 2014. "Citizenship and Punishment: The Salience of National Membership in U.S. Criminal Courts." *American Sociological Review* 79 (October): 825–47.

Lightning Reports. 2019. "Sheriff Hires First Latino Liaison. *Hendersonville Lightning*, June 4. www.hendersonvillelightning.com/four-seasons-politics/7969 -sheriff-hires-first-latino-liaison.html.

Liska, Allen E., and Mitchel B. Chamlin. 1984. "Social Structure and Crime Control among Macrosocial Units." *American Journal of Sociology* 90 (September): 383–95.

Locke, Mandy, and Danielle Battaglia. 2021. "Sheriffs Flex Muscle: A Powerful Lobby Shaped NC's Newest Body-Camera Law." *Gaston Gazette*, December 8. www.gastongazette.com/story/news/2021/12/08/nc-sheriffs-association-change -access-police-body-camera-law/6414431001/.

Longazel, Jamie G. 2013. "Moral Panic as Racial Degradation Ceremony: Racial Stratification and the Local-Level Backlash against Latino/a Immigrants." *Punishment and Society* 15 (January): 96–119.

———. 2014. "Rhetorical Barriers to Mobilizing for Immigrant Rights: White Innocence and Latina/o Abstraction." *Law and Social Inquiry* 39 (Summer): 580–600. doi:10.1111/lsi.12079.

Mann, Steven. 2010. "Demographic Trends of Hispanics/Latinos in North Carolina. Governor's Office of Hispanic/Latino Affairs. https://cnnc.uncg.edu/wp -content/uploads/2017/03/Demographic-trends-of-Latinos-in-NC-12-2011.pdf. Accessed October 24, 2022.

Marrow, Helen B. 2009. "New Immigrant Destinations and the American Colour Line." *Ethnic and Racial Studies* 32 (June): 1037–57.

Martinez, Lisa. 2005. "Yes We Can: Latino Participation in Unconventional Politics." *Social Forces* 84 (September): 135–55.

———. 2008. "The Individual and Contextual Determinants of Protest among Latinos." *Mobilization* 13 (June): 180–204.

Martinez, Ramiro, Jr. 2010. "Revisiting the Role of Latinos and Immigrants in Police Research." In *Race, Ethnicity, and Policing: New and Essential Readings*, edited by Stephen Rice and Michael White, 435–49. New York: New York University Press.

Marusak, Joe. 2018. "U.S. Sheriffs Crowdfunding for Border Wall: 'We Will Not Sit Idly By,' One in NC Says." *Charlotte Observer*, September 19. www.charlotte observer.com/news/local/crime/article218691170.html.

Massey, Douglas S. 2011. "The Past and Future of Mexico-U.S. Migration." In *Beyond La Frontera: The History of Mexico-U.S. Migration*, edited by Mark Overmyer-Velazquez, 241–65. New York: Oxford University Press.

Matias, Cheryl E. 2016. "White Skin, Black Friend: A Fanonian Application to

Theorize Racial Fetish in Teacher Education." *Educational Philosophy and Theory* 48 (January): 221–36.

Mayor's Immigration Study Commission. 2007. "Immigration: Legal and Illegal (Charlotte, NC)." January. https://localdocs.uncc.edu/Mayor/Reports_Studies/Immigration_Report.pdf.

Mayorkas, Alejandro. 2022. "Secretary Mayorkas Delivers Remarks at the U.S. Conference of Mayors." Department of Homeland Security, January 20. www.dhs.gov/news/2022/01/20/secretary-mayorkas-delivers-remarks-us-conference-mayors.

McAdam, Doug, Sidney Tarrow, and Charles Tilly. 2001. *Dynamics of Contention*. Cambridge: Cambridge University Press.

McDonald, Thomasi. 2012. "Illegal Immigration Strategy Shifts—U.S. Scales Back Using Local Police and Sheriff's Offices to Identify Offenders." *Raleigh News and Observer*, November 16. docs.newsbank.com/s/InfoWeb/aggdocs/AWNB/1429AD0F1A1FCA38/0D0CB4F32A21A855?p_multi=RLOB&s_lang=en-US. Accessed August 19, 2014. No longer available online.

———. 2018. "Activists Vow to Hold New Wake Sheriff Accountable on Promise to End Immigration Program." *Raleigh News and Observer*, November 8. www.newsobserver.com/news/local/article221359150.html.

———. 2019. "Amid an Uptick in Crime, a Coalition of Young Activists Pushed the Durham City Council Not to Hire More Cops." *Indyweek*, June 11. https://indyweek.com/news/durham/durham-beyond-policing-city-council-additional-officers-crime-wave/.

McDowell, Meghan G., and Nancy A. Wonders. 2009. "Keeping Migrants in Their Place: Technologies of Control and Racialized Public Space in Arizona." *Social Justice* 36, no. 2 (116): 54–72. http://www.jstor.org/stable/29768537.

McGoey, L. 2012. "The Logic of Strategic Ignorance." *British Journal of Sociology* 63 (September): 553–76.

Mecklenburg County BOC (Board of Commissioners). 2007. Meeting Minutes, August 14. https://www.mecknc.gov/CountyManagersOffice/BOCC/Meetings/Archived%20Meeting%20Minutes/2007%20Minutes.pdf.

Menjívar, Cecilia. 2014. "The 'Poli-Migra': Multilayered Legislation, Enforcement Practices, and What We Can Learn about and from Today's Approaches." *American Behavioral Scientist* 58 (November): 1805–19. doi: 10.1177/0002764214537268.

Menjívar, Cecilia, and Leisy J. Abrego. 2012a. "Legal Violence: Immigration Law and the Lives of Central American Immigrants." *American Journal of Sociology* 117 (March): 1380–421.

———. 2012b. "Legal Violence in the Lives of Immigrants: How Immigration Enforcement Affects Families, Schools, and Workplaces." Center for American Progress, December 11. www.americanprogress.org/article/legal-violence-in-the-lives-of-immigrants.

Miller, L. A., and V. W. Harris. 2018. "I Can't Be Racist—I Teach in an Urban School, and I'm a Nice White Lady!," *World Journal of Education* 8 (May): 1–11.

Mills, Charles W. 1997. *The Racial Contract*. Ithaca, N.Y.: Cornell University Press.

———. 2007. "White Ignorance." In *Race and Epistemologies of Ignorance*, edited by Shannon Sullivan and Nancy Tuana, 13–38. Albany: State University of New York Press.

Molina, Natalia. 2014. *How Race Is Made in America: Immigration, Citizenship, and the Historical Power of Racial Scripts*. Berkeley: University of California Press.

Montoya-Galvez, Camilo. 2022. "U.S. Expands "Remain in Mexico" Policy to Busiest Border Sector for Migrant Arrivals." CBS News, January 21. www.cbsnews.com /news/immigration-remain-in-mexico-policy-expand/.

Monzó, Lilia. 2015. "Ethnography in Charting Paths toward Persona and Social Liberation: Using My Latina Cultural Intuition." *International Journal of Qualitative Studies in Education* 28:373–93.

Moore, Wendy Leo, and Jennifer L. Pierce. 2007. "Still Killing Mockingbirds: Narratives of Race and Innocence in Hollywood's Depiction of the White Messiah Lawyer." *Qualitative Sociology Review* 3 (August): 171–87.

Moores, C. 2017. "Sen. Thom Tillis Talks Immigration with Iredell Farmers." *Statesville Record and Landmark*, March 12. www.statesville.com/news /sen-thom-tillis-talks-immigration-with-iredell-farmers/article_abof4576 -deb7-11e7-88c9-0733b8b24cfc.html.

Mora, Citlaly. 2019. "We Deserve to Live without Fear." ACLU of North Carolina, November 26. www.acluofnorthcarolina.org/en/news/we-deserve-live-without-fear.

Morales, Patricia. 2018. "A favor y en contra del 287g en foro de candidatos para sheriff." Que pasa media, January 10. https://quepasamedia.com/noticias /raleigh-durham/a-favor-y-en-contra-del-287g-en-foro-de-candidatos-para -sheriff/.

Morrill, Jim, and Michael Gordon. 2018. "ACLU Targets a Candidate—and a Program—with Big Money in Sheriff's Race. *Charlotte Observer*, May 4. www .charlotteobserver.com/news/politicsgovernment/election/article210296119 .html.

Mueller, J. C. 2017. "Producing Colorblindness: Everyday Mechanisms of White Ignorance." *Social Problems* 64 (May): 219–38.

Morrison, Aaron. 2019. "There's a Pattern of Police Unions Attacking People Who Call for Criminal Justice Reform, Especially When They Are Black." *Appeal*, November 27. https://theappeal.org/malcolm-jenkins-fraternal-order-police/.

Morse, Ann, Chesterfield Polkey, Lydia Deatherage, and Veronica Ibarra. 2019. "Sanctuary Policy FAQ." National Conference of State Legislatures. www.ncsl .org/research/immigration/sanctuary-policy-faq635991795.aspx.

Moss, Bill. 2013. "McDonald Announces Run for Sheriff." *Hendersonville Lightning*, August 27. www.hendersonvillelightning.com/politics/1973-mcdonald-announces -run-for-sheriff.html.

———. 2018. "Sheriff's Candidates Diverge on Training Center, Animal Control, Body Cams." *Hendersonville Lightning*, April 25. www.hendersonvillelightning .com/four-seasons-politics/6962-sheriff-s-candidates-diverge-on-training-center -animal-control-body-cams.html.

National Sheriffs' Association. 2019. "Sheriffs Deliver Letter Supporting ICE

Funding to Capitol Hill." www.sheriffs.org/Sheriffs-Deliver-Letter-Supporting -ICE-Funding-Capitol-Hill. Accessed October 24, 2022.

NCDPS (North Carolina Department of Public Safety Division of Adult Correction and Juvenile Justice). 2016. "Community Corrections Policy & Procedures." In author's possession.

NDLON (National Day Labor Organizing Network). 2016. "Breaking: DHS, ICE, and DOJ Sued in Federal Court Over Controversial Deportation Program," January 19. https://ndlon.org/breaking-dhs-ice-and-doj-sued-in-federal-court-over -controversial-deportation-program/.

Nguyen, Mai Thi, and Hannah Gill. 2010. "The 287 (g) Program: The Costs and Consequences of Local Immigration Enforcement in North Carolina Communities." Latino Migration Project, February. http://cgi.unc.edu/uploads/media _items/287g-report-final.original.pdf. Accessed November 15, 2015.

Nichanian, Daniel. 2018. "How Tuesday's Sheriff Elections Dealt a Blow to ICE." Appeal, November 8. https://theappeal.org/how-tuesdays-sheriff-elections -dealt-a-blow-to-ice/.

———. 2019. "Illinois Banned a Prized ICE Program. Why Are So Few Blue States Doing the Same?" Appeal, September 16. https://theappeal.org/illinois-banned -a-prized-ice-program-why-are-so-few-blue-states-doing-the-same/.

Nik, Theodore, et al. 2013. "Insecure Communities: Latino Perceptions of Police Involvement in Immigration Enforcement." PolicyLink, May. www.policylink .org/sites/default/files/INSECURE_COMMUNITIES_REPORT_FINAL.PDF.

North Carolina State Bureau of Investigation. 2009. "Memorandum of Agreement." www.ice.gov/doclib/foia/secure_communities-moa/r_north_carolina_10-23-09 .pdf.

Odem, M. E. 2016." Immigration Politics in the New Latino South." *Journal of American Ethnic History* 35 (Spring): 87–91.

Office of the Sheriff in North Carolina. 2014. https://ncsheriffs.org/wp-content /uploads/2015/01/The_Office_of_Sheriff_in_North_Carolina-Sept152014.pdf.

Oliver, Willard M. 2006. "The Fourth Era of Policing: Homeland Security." *International Review of Law, Computers and Technology* 20 (March–July): 49–62.

Ordonez, Franco. 2008. "Pendergraph Quits Federal Position." *Charlotte Observer*, August 26. Accessed August 19, 2014. No longer available online.

———. 2012. "Passionate Advocacy Marked Myrick's Tenure—Myrick's Outspoken Conservatism Made Friends, Foes." *Raleigh News and Observer*, December 30. http://docs.newsbank.com/s/InfoWeb/aggdocs/AWNB/14386C7525256E10/0DoC B4F32A21A855?p_multi=RLOB&s_lang=en-US. Accessed August 19, 2014. No longer available online.

Pedroza, Juan Manuel. 2013. "Removal Roulette: Secure Communities and Immigration Enforcement in the United States (2008–2012)." In *Outside Justice: Immigration and the Criminalizing Impact of Changing Policy and Practice*, edited by David C Brotherton, Daniel L Stageman, and Shirley P. Leyro, 45–65. New York: Springer New York. doi:10.1007/978-1-4614-6648-2_3.

People's Alliance. 2014. Fall 2014 Endorsements. www.durhampa.org/fall_2014 _endorsements.

Pew Research Center. 2014. "Demographic Profile of Hispanics in North Carolina," www.pewhispanic.org/states/state/nc/. Accessed February 13, 2017.

Pinkerton, James, and St. John Barned-Smith. 2017. "Sheriff Cuts Ties with ICE Program over Immigrant Detention. *Houston Chronicle*, February 21. www .houstonchronicle.com/news/houston-texas/houston/article/Sheriff-cuts-ties -with-ICE-program-over-immigrant-10949617.php.

Pinto, Nick. 2020. "Across the US, Trump Used ICE to Crack Down on Immigration Activists." *Intercept*, November 1. https://theintercept.com/2020/11/01/ice -immigration-activists-map/.

Polletta, Francesca. 2012. *Freedom Is an Endless Meeting: Democracy in American Social Movements*. Chicago: University of Chicago Press.

Powers, Ashley. 2018. "The Renegade Sheriffs: A Law-Enforcement Movement That Claims to Answer Only to the Constitution." *New Yorker*, April 30. www .newyorker.com/magazine/2018/04/30/the-renegade-sheriffs.

Price, David. 2019. "After North Carolina Immigration Raids, Price Pushes to End Heartless Enforcement Policies." https://price.house.gov/newsroom/press -releases/after-north-carolina-immigration-raids-price-pushes-end-heartless.

Prieto, G. 2016. "Opportunity, Threat, and Tactics: Collaboration and Confron- tation by Latino Immigrant Challengers." In *Narratives of Identity in Social Movements, Conflicts and Change*. Vol. 40, edited by Landon E. Hancock. Bingley, Eng.: Emerald Group. https://doi-org.proxy006.nclive.org/10.1108/s0163 -786x20160000040005.

Provine, Marie Doris, Monica W. Varsanyi, Paul G. Lewis, and Scott H. Decker. 2016. *Policing Immigrants: Local Law Enforcement on the Front Lines*. Chicago: University of Chicago Press.

Ramakrishnan, S. Karthick, and Paul Lewis. 2005. *Immigrants and Local Governance: The View from City Hall*. San Francisco: Public Policy Institute of California.

Ramakrishnan, S. Karthick, and Tom (Tak) Wong. 2007. "Immigration Policies Go Local: The Varying Responses of Local Governments to Undocumented Immi- gration." Unpublished manuscript.

Ray, Victor E., Pamela Herd, and Donald Moynihan. 2020. "Racialized Burdens: Applying Racialized Organization Theory to the Administrative State." SocArXiv, December 9. doi:10.31235/osf.io/q3xb8.

Redaccion La Voz. 2018. "Muy Pocos Hispanos Votaron en Henderson." *La Voz Independiente*.

Robbins, M. D., B. Simonsen, and B. Feldman. 2008. "Citizens and Resource Allo- cation: Improving Decision Making with Interactive Web-Based Citizen Partici- pation." *Public Administration Review* 68 (March): 564–75.

Roediger, D. 2007. *The Wages of Whiteness: Race and the Making of the American Working Class*. Brooklyn, NY: Verso.

Romero, Mary. 2008. "Crossing the Immigration and Race Border: A Critical Race Theory Approach to Immigration Studies." *Contemporary Justice Review* 11 (June): 23–37.

Ross, Thomas. 1990. "The Rhetorical Tapestry of Race: White Innocence and Black Abstraction." *William and Mary Law Review* 32 (Fall): 1–40.

Russell-Brown, Katheryn. 2009. *The Color of Crime*. 2nd ed. Critical America. New York: New York University Press.

Sáenz, Rogelio, and Karen Manges Douglas. 2015. "A Call for the Racialization of Immigration Studies: On the Transition of Ethnic Immigrants to Racialized Immigrants." *Sociology of Race and Ethnicity* 1 (January): 168–80.

Schriro, Dora, B. 2009. "Homeland Security, Immigration and Customs Enforcement, Immigrant Detention Overview and Recommendations." October 6. www.ice.gov/doclib/about/offices/odpp/pdf/ice-detention-rpt.pdf .

Schultz, Mark. 2018. "Durham County Sheriff Rejects Call to Stop Honoring ICE Detainers." *Herald Sun*, May 8. www.heraldsun.com/news/local/counties /durham-county/article210596544.html.

Seawright, Jason. 2008. "Case Selection Techniques in Case Study Research: A Menu of Qualitative and Quantitative Options." *Political Research Quarterly* 61 (June): 294–308.

Shaffer, J. 2018. "With Focus on Immigration, Voters in NC's Seven Largest Counties Elected Black Sheriffs." *Charlotte Observer*, November 8. www.charlotte observer.com/news/local/article221343255.html.

Shepherd, Katie. 2018. "Sheriff Mike Reese Refuses to Provide Reports to ICE. But Others Do It behind His Back." *Williamette Week*, August 29. www.wweek.com /news/courts/2018/08/29/sheriff-mike-reese-refuses-to-provide-reports-to-ice-but -others-do-it-behind-his-back/.

Smith, Nickelle. 2019. "New Liaison Talks Immigration Relations in Henderson Co." WSPA News, June 25. www.wspa.com/news/new-liaison-talks-immigrant -relations-in-henderson-co/.

Snow, David, and Danny Trom. 2002. "The Case Study and the Study of Social Movements." *Methods of Social Movement Research*, edited by Bert Klandermans and Suzanne Staggenborg, 146–72. Minneapolis: University of Minnesota Press.

Spear, Susie. 2019. "State and Local Dems Question Sheriff's Role as Trump Campaign's State Chair." *News and Record*, July 26. https://greensboro.com /rockingham_now/news/state-and-local-dems-question-sheriffs-role-as-trump -campaigns-state-chair/article_a0f9f74c-12ec-5d2c-85ca-41bf41f1b5a4.html.

Specht, Paul. 2018. "After Rant Surfaces about 'Mexicans,' NC Democrat Drops Out of House Race." *Raleigh News and Observer*, July 25. www.newsobserver.com /news/politics-government/article215502285.html.

SPLC (Southern Poverty Law Center). 2017. "Union Sues North Carolina over Law Stripping Rights from 100,000 Farmworkers." November 15. www.splcenter.org /news/2017/11/15/union-sues-north-carolina-over-law-stripping-rights-100000 -farmworkers.

Staff Reports. 2018a. "Elections 2018: Cabarrus County Sheriff Republican Candidates." *Independent Tribune*, April 23. www.independenttribune.com/news /elections-cabarrus-county-sheriff-republican-candidates/article_defa0410-4722 -11e8-8f98-1f87280a8f5d.html.

———. 2018b. "Shaw Wins Sheriff Republican Primary." *Independent Tribune*, May 8. www.independenttribune.com/news/shaw-wins-sheriff-republican -primary/article_29dbd9ca-5337-11e8-92eb-abbbc9569289.html.

———. 2018c. "Shaw Pulls Out Sheriff Race." *Independent Tribune*, November 6. www.independenttribune.com/news/shaw-pulls-out-sheriff-race/article _3a6ae268-e248-11e8-8a63-0fad204fc9f3.html.

St. Onge, Peter. 2006. "An Eye on Illegal Immigrants." *Raleigh News and Observer*, December 10. http://docs.newsbank.com/s/InfoWeb/aggdocs/AWNB/115EFB2EC1 D8BF70/0D0CB4F32A21A855?p_multi=RLOB&s_lang=en-US. Accessed August 19, 2014. No longer available online.

Stuart, F. 2011. "Race, Space, and the Regulation of Surplus Labor: Policing African-Americans in Los Angeles' Skid Row." *Souls: A Critical Journal of Black Politics, Culture, and Society* 13 (April–June): 197–212.

Stuesse, Angela, and Mathew Coleman. 2014. "Automobility, Immobility, Alter-mobility: Surviving and Resisting the Intensification of Immigrant Policing." *City and Society* 26 (April): 51–72.

Stumpf, Juliet P. 2006. "The Crimmigration Crisis: Immigrants, Crime, and Sover-eign Power." *American University Law Review* 56 (December): 367–420.

Tarrow, Sidney G. 2011. *Power in Movement: Social Movements and Contentious Pol-itics*. Rev. and updated 3rd ed. Cambridge Studies in Comparative Politics. New York: Cambridge University Press.

Tauss, Leigh. 2018. "Wake County's Incoming Sheriff Has Pledged to End 287(g). That Won't Help Camilo Coronilla Loyola." *IndyWeek*. https://indyweek.com /news/wake/wake-county-287-gerald-baker/.

Taylor, Keeanga-Yamahtta. 2021. "The Bitter Fruits of Trump's White-Power Presi-dency." *New Yorker*, January 12. www.newyorker.com/news/our-columnists /the-bitter-fruits-of-trumps-white-power-presidency.

Taylor, Marylee. 1998. "How White Attitudes Vary with the Racial Composition of Local Populations: Numbers Count." *American Sociological Review* 63 (August): 512–35.

Terry, Dana, Amanda Magnus, and Frank Stasio. 2019. "Western NC Reacts To ICE's 'New Normal.'" *The State of Things*, March 7. www.wunc.org/show/the-state -of-things/2019-03-07/western-nc-reacts-to-ices-new-normal.

Thompson, Daniel. 2020. "How Partisan Is Local Law Enforcement? Evidence from Sheriff Cooperation with Immigration Authorities." *American Political Science Review* 114 (November): 222–36.

TRAC (Transactional Records Access Clearinghouse). n.d.-a. "Latest Data: Immi-gration and Customs Enforcement Detainers." http://trac.syr.edu/phptools /immigration/detain/. Accessed October 28, 2022.

———. n.d.-b. "Intergovernmental Service Agreement (IGSA) Facility." http://trac .syr.edu/immigration/reports/222/. Accessed October 28, 2022.

———. 2017. "ICE Refuses To Release More Comprehensive Detainer Data." March 20. https://trac.syr.edu/whatsnew/email.170320.html.

UNC School of Law Immigration/Human Rights Policy Clinic and ASISTA. 2019. "Visa Denied: The Political Geography of the U Visa: Eligibility as a Matter of Locale." https://law.unc.edu/wp-content/uploads/2019/10/uvisafullreport.pdf.

U.S. Department of Homeland Security. 2014. Priority Enforcement Program Memo. www.dhs.gov/sites/default/files/publications/14_1120_memo _prosecutorial_discretion.pdf.

U.S. Department of Homeland Security Immigration and Customs Enforcement and North Carolina State Bureau of Investigation. 2009. "Memorandum of Agreement." www.ice.gov/doclib/foia/secure_communities-moa/r_north _carolina_10-23-09.pdf.

Vargas, Robert, and Philip McHarris. 2017. "Race and State in City Police Spending Growth: 1980 to 2010." *Sociology of Race and Ethnicity* 3 (January): 96–112.

Varsanyi, Monica W., Paul G. Lewis, Doris Marie Provine, and Scott Decker. 2012. "A Multilayered Jurisdictional Patchwork: Immigration Federalism in the United States." *Law and Policy* 34 (December): 138–58.

Vasquez, Tina. 2017. "ICE Report on So-Called Safety Threats 'Misleading at Best.'" *Rewire*, March 22. https://rewire.news/article/2017/03/22/ice-report-so-called -safety-threats-misleading-best/.

Vázquez, Yolanda. 2015. "Constructing Crimmigration: Latino Subordination in a Post-racial World." *Ohio State Law Journal* 76 (June): 599–658.

Vera, Hernan, and Andrew Gordon. 2003. *Screen Saviors: Hollywood Fictions of Whiteness*. Lanham, Md.: Rowman and Littlefield.

Verba, Sidney, Key Lehman Schlozman, and Henry E. Brady. 1995. *Voice and Equality: Civic Voluntarism in American Politics*. Cambridge, Mass.: Harvard University Press.

Wacquant. Loïc. 2009. *Punishing the Poor: The Neoliberal Government of Social Insecurity*. Durham, N.C.: Duke University Press.

———. 2010. "Crafting the Neoliberal State: Workfare, Prisonfare, and Social Insecurity." *Sociological Forum* 25 (June): 197–220.

Wake County BOC (Board of Commissioners). 2008. "September 15, 2008, Regular Meeting." Video. https://wake.granicus.com/MediaPlayer.php?view_id=&clip _id=285&meta_id=19087.

Wallace-Wells, Benjamine. 2018. "The A.C.L.U. Is Getting Involved in Elections— and Reinventing Itself for the Trump Era." *New Yorker*, June 8. www.newyorker .com/news/news-desk/the-aclu-is-getting-involved-in-elections-and-reinventing -itself-for-the-trump-era.

WBTV. 2017. "Speakers Protest Idea of ICE Agents Policing Mecklenburg Commissioners' Meeting." March 8. www.wbtv.com/story/34692399/speakers-protest -idea-of-ice-agents-policing-mecklenburg-commissioners-meeting/.

Web Staff. 2019. "Rockingham County Sheriff Promotes Crowdfunding Effort to Fund Mexico Border Wall." MyFox8, September 19. https://myfox8.com/2018/09/19 /rockingham-county-sheriff-promotes-crowdfunding-effort-to-fund-mexico -border-wall/.

Weeks, Gregory. 2009. "A Highly Flawed but Fixable Program." *Raleigh News and*

*Observer*, March 26. http://docs.newsbank.com/s/InfoWeb/aggdocs/AWNB/1272
ED55A852D488/0D0CB4F32A21A855?p_multi=RLOB&s_lang=en-US. Accessed
August 19, 2014. No longer available online.

Weise, Julie M. 2015. *Corazón de Dixie: Mexicanos in the U.S. South since 1910*.
David J. Weber Series in the New Borderlands History. Chapel Hill: University of
North Carolina Press.

Weitzer, Ronald. 2013. "The Puzzling Neglect of Hispanic Americans in Research
on Police–Citizen Relations." *Ethnic and Racial Studies* 37 (May): 1995–2013.

Willets, Sarah. 2017a. "ICE's Explanation for Rounding Up Immigrants at Duke
Manor Tuesday: He was There." *IndyWeek*, March 29. www.indyweek.com/news
/archives/2017/03/29/ices-explanation-for-rounding-up-immigrant-at-duke
-manor-this-morning-he-was-there.

———. 2017b. "Does the Durham County Sheriff's Office Participate in ICE's Secure
Communities Program? It Says No. The Facts Say . . . Probably." *Indyweek*,
June15. https://indyweek.com/news/archives/durham-county-sheriff-s-office
-participate-ice-s-secure-communities-program-says-no.-facts-say-...-probably./.

———. 2018. Durham County's Friendly Relationship with ICE Could Hinge on Its
Sheriff's Reelection Bid. *IndyWeek*, March 21. www.indyweek.com/indyweek
/durham-countys-friendly-relationship-with-ice-could-hinge-on-its-sheriffs
-reelection-bid/Content?oid=12522569.

———. 2019. "NC Sheriff's Association Comes Out against Bill Requiring Cooperation with ICE." *Indyweek*, April 3.www.indyweek.com/news/northcarolina/nc
-sheriff-s-association-comes-out-against-bill-requiring-co/.

Winant, H. 2004. "Behind Blue Eyes: Whiteness and Contemporary U.S. Racial Politics." In *Off White: Readings on Power, Privilege, and Resistance*, 2nd ed., edited
by M. Fine, L. Weis, L. P. Pruitt, and A. Burns, 3–16. New York: Routledge.

Winders, Jamie. 2007. "Bringing Back the (B)order: Post-9/11 Politics of Immigration, Borders, and Belonging in the Contemporary US South." *Antipode* 39
(December): 920–42.

Wong, Tom K. "287(g) and the Politics of Interior Immigration Control in the
United States: Explaining Local Cooperation with Federal Immigration Authorities." *Journal of Ethnic and Migration Studies* 38, no. 5 (May 2012): 737–56.

Wootson, Cleve, R., and Ann D. Helms. 2007. "Detention Center Sought for Aliens."
*Raleigh News and Observer*, August 16. http://docs.newsbank.com/s/InfoWeb
/aggdocs/AWNB/11B10942B054DD20/0D0CB4F32A21A855?p_multi=RLOB&s
_lang=en-US. Accessed August 19, 2014. No longer available online.

WOSC-TV News. 2018. "New Sheriff in Town: McFadden Ousts Carmichael in Meck
County." May 9. www.wsoctv.com/news/local/vote-2018-mecklenburg-county
-sheriff-race/742846556.

Yost, Scott. 2018. "Mass Firings at Sheriff Office." *Rhino Times*, November 28. www
.rhinotimes.com/news/mass-firings-at-sheriffs-department/.

Zepeda-Millán, Chris. 2017. *Latino Mass Mobilization: Immigration, Racialization,
and Activism*. Cambridge: Cambridge University Press.

Printed in the USA
CPSIA information can be obtained
at www.ICGtesting.com
CBHW020354230224
4624CB00001B/42